The Victorious Church

In the Book of Revelation

A Commentary and Questions

Revised Edition

Lucian Farrar, Jr.

James Kay Publishing

Tulsa, Oklahoma

The Victorious Church
In the Book of Revelation
ISBN 978-1-943245-00-0

www.jameskaypublishing.com

e-mail: sales@jameskaypublishing.com

© 2006, 2016 Lucian Farrar, Jr.
Over 1,000 copies of the 2006 Edition are in circulation.
Cover design by JKP
Author Photo by Bob Cooper

2.3
All rights reserved.
No part of this book may be reproduced in any form or by any means
— except for review questions or brief quotations —
without permission in writing from the author.

also by
Lucian Farrar, Jr.

The Book of Daniel
The Most High Rules
A Commentary and Questions

The Book of Isaiah
Christ, Our Redeemer
A Commentary and Questions

The Minor Prophets
God's Spokesmen
A Commentary and Questions

Psalms – Book 1
David's Original Collection

Psalms – Books 2 & 3
Psalms 42 - 89

The Life of Christ
A Chronological Account

Scriptures are from the King James Version with archaic words, forms, and punctuations replaced by those in current use.

Other translations are acknowledged by the following abbreviations:

ASV – American Standard Version
ESV – English Standard Version
NASB – New American Standard Bible, 1973 Edition
NIV – New International Version, 1996 Edition
NKJV – New King James Version

Dedication

This book is dedicated to the memory of my parents:

Lucian M. Farrar and **Anna Mae (Smith) Farrar**

When I was a young child, my mother gave me a basic knowledge of both the Old and New Testaments by her vivid reading of Bible stories—she made them come alive. My desire to know the truth as revealed in the Scriptures was inspired by the example and the preaching of my father. Before his nineteenth birthday, he had read the entire Bible three times. Understanding the gospel of Christ, he obeyed it and dedicated his life to proclaiming Jesus Christ as Lord and Savior. He emphasized the need to know the truth revealed in the Bible. "And you shall know the truth, and the truth shall make you free." (John 8:32) During his ministry of 46 years, he preached in Tennessee, Kentucky, Mississippi, New Mexico, Texas, and Arkansas. My interest in knowing and understanding the Scriptures, I owe to my parents.

— Lucian Farrar, Jr.

Thank You

My appreciation goes to Jeff Taylor and Bob Colvin for their proof reading this book and to Derek Bullard for making all the corrections.

Table of Contents

Dedication ix

An Introduction to Revelation 1

View 1: The Seven Lampstands 5
Christ with His Church, Chapter 1 7
The Seven Letters, Chapters 2 - 3 19

View 2: The Seven Seals 39
The Open Door in Heaven, Chapters 4 - 5 41
The Seven Seals, Chapters 6 - 7 51

View 3: The Seven Trumpets 67
The Seven Trumpets, Chapters 8 - 9 69
The Little Book, Chapters 10 - 11 79

View 4: The Victorious Lamb 93
The Woman & the Dragon, Chapter 12 95
The Two Beasts & The Lamb, Chapters 13 - 14 105

View 5: The Seven Bowls of Wrath 123
The Seven Bowls of Wrath, Chapters 15 - 16 125

View 6: The Marriage of the Lamb 143
Babylon and the Beast, Chapter 17 145
God Almighty Reigns, Chapters 18 - 19 161

View 7: The Victorious Church 175
The Millennium & The Judgment, Chapter 20 177
The Victorious Church, Chapters 21 - 22 191

The Unity of Revelation 211

Bibliography 213

An Introduction to Revelation

My interest in the book of Revelation began in the summer of 1959, when I was nineteen years old. I was selling Bibles in Atlanta, Georgia, and someone asked me about the two resurrections in Revelation 20:4-6. I told him that I knew of only one resurrection. Jesus had said, "The hour is coming, in which all that are in the graves shall hear his voice and shall come forth." (John 5:28-29) While rejecting his belief in two literal resurrections separated by 1,000 years, I wanted to know the meaning of Revelation 20:4-6. After returning to Harding College in Searcy, Arkansas that fall, I asked one of my Bible teachers about this, and he gave me a paper that he had written on Revelation 20. These two resurrections are not literal bodily resurrections but are symbolic and spiritual like the one in Ezekiel 37:1-14.

During my senior year in college, I preached on Sundays at Bells Chapel near Atkins, Arkansas. Our Bible class was studying the Book of Revelation using a very helpful workbook by Granville Tyler. To answer the questions required reading each chapter four times. I learned that Revelation interprets many of its symbols.

I became determined to discover the meaning of the figurative language in Revelation and to understand its message. I studied various commentaries, encyclopedias, dictionaries, Greek lexicons, and history books. I have used the inductive method of hermeneutics by seeking to gather all the facts before drawing a conclusion. Any interpretation that does not agree with all the facts has been ruled out. Harmony is a basic demand of truth. My approach to Revelation is a combination of the historical method and the philosophy of history interpretation.[1]

---

[1] Ray Summers, *Worthy is the Lamb,* pp. 45-46

Revelation describes the persecutor of God's servants as a ***beast*** that comes up out of the sea in 13:1. The beast has seven heads that represent seven kings or kingdoms: "five are fallen, and one is, and the other has not yet come." (17:7-10) Some commentaries limit this beast to the Roman Empire. They interpret the seven heads to be the first seven Roman emperors to establish a throne, and the beast is Domitian, the eighth Roman emperor. This approach has many problems.

First, only two of these eight emperors, Nero and Domitian, brought severe persecutions against the church. The other six emperors were not of the beast. Christians were protected under their rule, as seen in Acts 19:23-41, Acts 21:30-40, and Acts 23:12-35.

Second, this view does not agree with the time when the book was written. This popular view states that the five fallen heads are the first five Roman emperors. The next three are omitted because each one ruled for only a few months; but they were not able to establish their thrones. Vespasian is said to be the one who *is*, and therefore he would be the emperor when Revelation was written. Titus would be the seventh emperor, and Domitian the eighth. However, this does not agree with Irenaeus, who testified in the second century that the book was written "at the end of Domitian's reign."[2]

Third, John was in **"the tribulation"** when the book was written. (1:9) If the seven heads were the first seven Roman emperors, the book was written during the reign of Vespasian. But F. W. Mattox states in his church history, "Under Vespasian (69-79) there is no record of Christians suffering for their faith."[3] Vespasian's reign does not fit the conditions when the book was written,

---

[2] Paul L. Maier, *Eusebius—The Church History*, p. 107
[3] F. W. Mattox, *The Eternal Kingdom*, p. 9

but the reign of Domitian does. The early church historian Eusebius gave this testimony: "With terrible cruelty, Domitian ... showed himself Nero's successor in hostility to God. He was the second to organize a persecution against us, though his father, Vespasian, had no such evil plans." [4]

Frank Pack observes, "Any endeavor to make the heads correspond to the Roman emperors runs into difficulty."[5]

Fourth, this view does not agree with the context of Revelation. The victors over the beast in Revelation 15:2 are not just singing *"the song of the Lamb."* They also are singing *"the song of Moses."* This takes us back to Israel's victory over the Egyptians at the Red Sea. The first fallen head is Pharaoh and the Egyptians. God's faithful servants were singing the song of Moses and the song of the Lamb because they had the victory over the Egyptians as well as the Romans.

Though Revelation was written primarily to first century Christians, its message is not limited to the first century. For example, the writer of Hebrews exhorted first century Christians to be faithful by reviewing great heroes of faith who lived during the Old Testament times.[6] In a similar way, Revelation gives hope to Christians who are being persecuted by reminding them of God's victories over great kingdoms in the past.

The five fallen kingdoms are those of the Egyptians, the Assyrians, the Babylonians, the Medes & Persians, and the Greeks. The sixth kingdom is the Roman Empire, the one that *is*. The ten horns belong to the sixth head, the Romans. The seventh head represents any future persecutor

---

[4] Paul L. Maier, *Eusebius—The Church History*, p. 104
[5] Frank Pack, *Revelation, Part 2*, p. 32, Sweet Publishing Co.
[6] Hebrews 11:4 – 12:1

after the Romans, for at that time he had "not yet come." The beast is made up of all persecutors of God's people. He "is of the seven, and goes into perdition." (17:11) God has destroyed the kingdoms of those powerful rulers that have persecuted his people. Such knowledge should bring comfort to Christians whenever and wherever they suffer "for the testimony of Jesus Christ." (1:9)

The persecution by the Romans was not continuous. *The Wall Chart of World History* by Professor Edward Hull shows ten red crosses which denote the Ten Great Persecutions of the Christians by the Roman Empire.[7] Kenneth Scott Latourette, a professor at Yale University, wrote, "Usually ten major persecutions are enumerated, beginning with Nero in the first century and culminating in the one which was inaugurated by Diocletian early in the fourth century."[8] These ten periods of persecution are predicted by the "ten days" of tribulation in Revelation 2:10. Several commentaries view the time of the Roman Empire as one long period of continuous persecution, but this is not true. During the 249 years that span these persecutions, Christians suffered severely for only 49 years. Mattox describes the period before the tenth persecution with these words: "From 260 to 303 there was no persecution by authority of the state. During this period the church grew rapidly."[9]

You are encouraged to use your Bible as you study this commentary. You will gain a better understanding of the book by looking up the references to the Scriptures that are in the comments and footnotes. Remember, all the facts must agree, or the interpretation is wrong. May God bless you in your search for the truth.

---

[7] Edward Hull, *The Wall Chart of World History*, Dorset Press, 1988
[8] Kenneth Scott Latourette, *A History of Christianity*, p. 85
[9] F. W. Mattox, *The Eternal Kingdom*, p. 97

View 1

The Seven Lampstands

Revelation 1 – 3

NOTES

Christ with His Church
Revelation 1

John is a prisoner. He has been banished to an island for preaching the word of God and for confessing that Jesus is the Lord. It is Sunday, the Lord's Day. Suddenly, he hears a loud voice behind him, and he turns to see an awesome vision! He sees Jesus, the Son of Man, in a glorified appearance, walking among seven golden lampstands. His eyes are like flaming fire. And out of his mouth is a sharp two-edged sword. His face is shining like the sun. John is overcome by the sight, and falls at the feet of Jesus. But Jesus Christ lays his right hand on him and says, "Fear not."

Revelation was written to comfort Christians who were suffering persecutions by the Romans and the Jews. Jesus has a message of blessed assurance for his church, "Do not be afraid."

The Church is victorious with Christ the King! This is the theme of the book. **Ten Roman kings** *shall make war with the Lamb, and the Lamb shall overcome them, for he is the Lord of lords and King of kings; and they that are with him are called, and chosen, and faithful.* **(17:14)**

The victorious Lamb is Jesus Christ, the rider on the white horse.[10] He conquers with the gospel. And those that are with him are true Christians, because they are *called* by the gospel, they are *chosen*, and they are "*faithful* unto death."[11]

---

[10] Revelation 6:2, Revelation 19:11-16, Revelation 1:16
[11] 2 Thessalonians 2:13-14, 1 Peter 2:9, Revelation 2:10

The Revelation of Jesus Christ, which God gave to him…and he sent and signified it by his angel to his servant John. **1:1** *Apocalypses* is the Greek word for revelation, meaning an uncovering of things before unknown. Because of this, the book is also known as The Apocalypse. The heavenly Father is the author, who gave the Revelation to Jesus Christ. The focus is on Christ. He is the one who opens the book that reveals God's plan for the future in 5:1-9. His angel is the messenger. The apostle John is the writer. He was so well known in the early church he could refer to himself simply as "John." Early writers who identify him as John the apostle include Justin Martyr (AD 140), Irenaeus (180), and Clement of Alexandria (200).

The Revelation was given ***to show to his servants things which must shortly come to pass.*** **1:1** Many of the predictions in this book were to be fulfilled soon after they were written. For example, John would be released from his island prison within a year. (10:11)

John ***bore record of the word of God, and the testimony of Jesus Christ, and of all things that he saw.*** **1:2** He saw wonderful visions. He heard the testimony of Jesus and of the angels. John wrote about all the things that he had seen and heard. (1:19)

Blessed is he that reads and they that hear the words of this prophecy and keep those things which are written therein: for the time is at hand. **1:3** If most of the predictions in this book were to be fulfilled 500 to 2,000 years later, the first readers could not have been blessed by reading it. Predictions about Muhammad, the Pope, or the twenty-first century European Union would have been meaningless to them. These early Christians were to experience the things revealed. The symbolism had meaning for them. The time was near for these prophecies to be fulfilled.

Revelation was written *to the seven churches which are in Asia.* **1:4** The Roman province of Asia was located in what is western Turkey today. These seven churches were not seven denominations with different creeds. They were congregations of Christ's one church in seven cities: Ephesus, Smyrna, Pergamos, Thyatira, Sardis, Philadelphia, and Laodicea. (1:11) What did this book mean to them? Just as we can learn from Paul's letters to churches and individuals in the first century, we also can be blessed by the book of Revelation whenever we can apply its instructions to our own lives.

Some put the date for the writing of Revelation before Jerusalem was destroyed in AD 70.[12] However, the evidence from early church writers places the date around AD 95. Polycarp of Smyrna had been taught by the apostle John to whom the Revelation had been given.[13] As a youth, Irenaeus was converted to Christ by the teachings of Polycarp.[14] Irenaeus testified in his second century writings that the Revelation was written "at the end of Domitian's reign."[15] Domitian was the Roman Emperor from AD 81 to 96, and he was known for his cruel persecution of Christians.[16] Therefore, Revelation was written about AD 95.

The Revelation is from three persons: *from him which is, and which was, and which is to come; and from the seven Spirits which are before his throne; and from Jesus Christ.* **1:4-5.** God the Father is the Lord, "the one which is, and which was, and which is to come, the Almighty." (1:8) He is the first person. Jesus Christ is named as the third person. Therefore, the second

---

[12] Foy E. Wallace, Jr., *The Book of Revelation,* p.16
[13] F. F. Bruce, *The Spreading Flame,* p. 174
[14] F. W. Mattox, *The Eternal Kingdom,* p. 78
[15] Paul L. Maier, *Eusebius—The Church History,* p. 107
[16] F. W. Mattox, *The Eternal Kingdom,* p. 93

person, who is called "the seven Spirits," must be the Holy Spirit. He is the complete, perfect Spirit, being symbolized by the number seven. The doctrine of the Trinity—three persons in one God—is taught here in Revelation 1:5. Jesus Christ is *the faithful witness*—we can believe his testimony, *the first begotten of the dead*—the first to be raised not to die again, and *the prince of the kings of the earth.* **1:5** Christ now has all power and authority. (Matthew 28:18)

Our Lord Jesus Christ *loved us and washed us from our sins in his own blood.* **1:5** He shed his blood "for the remission of sins." (Matthew 26:28) We are to "be baptized for the remission of sins." (Acts 2:38) We are "baptized into his death" where his blood was shed. (Romans 6:3) Our sins are washed away in his blood when we are baptized into Christ. (Acts 22:16) Then as Christians, his blood cleanses us from all sins when we walk in the light and confess our sins. (1 John 1:7-9)

Christ *has made us kings and priests unto his God and his Father.* **1:6** The New American Standard Bible reads, he "has made us a kingdom, priests to His God." Those who have been saved by the blood of Christ have been translated into the kingdom of Christ. (Colossians 1:13-14) We may be considered lesser kings upon thrones when we teach the gospel to others, live the Christian life, and endure the trials of our faith. Christians are now serving as priests to God in "a royal priesthood." (1 Peter 2:5, 9) If we are now priests, we are also now in the kingdom. Revelation 1:6 says that he **has made** us a kingdom—past tense, not future tense. We are now a kingdom and priests to God.

Behold, he comes with clouds. **1:7** This promise was made also by the angels when Jesus ascended through a cloud into heaven at the end of his earthly ministry. (Acts 1:9-11) *And every eye shall see him, and* *they also which pierced him.* **1:7** When Christ comes again, he will be visible to all. The teaching that Christ will have a secret return, known only to a few, must be false. Even those who crucified Jesus will be raised and see him. Thus, the doctrine of the rapture is also false, because it states that only the righteous dead will be raised at his coming.

I am Alpha and Omega, the beginning and the ending, says the Lord, who is, and who was, and who is to come, the Almighty. **1:8** God has power to create and finish all things; he is eternal.

In **1:9**, John describes himself as being a spiritual **brother and companion** with first century Christians in three things. *First*, they were **in the tribulation**. The definite article (the) is in the Greek text. The tribulation was then. *Second*, they were **in the kingdom** of Jesus Christ. The kingdom was in existence at that time. Any teaching that says the kingdom of Christ has not come is false in light of Revelation 1:9. *Third*, they were **in the patience of Jesus Christ**. John and his fellow Christians could endure the tribulation with courage because they knew they were in the kingdom of Christ and because they were following the example of perseverance and patience set by Jesus, who was steadfast to the end. (Rev. 14:12; and Hebrews 12:1-2)

John *was in the isle that is called Patmos, for the word of God, and for the testimony of Jesus Christ.* **1:9** Patmos is a small rocky island in the Aegean Sea, located 70 miles from Ephesus. John was exiled there in AD 95, the fourteenth year of the reign of Domitian, and he returned to Ephesus in AD 96 under the emperor Nerva.[17] John was suffering for preaching the word of God and confessing that Jesus is Lord.

---

[17] *International Standard Bible Encyclopaedia*, Vol. IV, p. 2263

John *was in the Spirit on the Lord's Day.* 1:10 He was not referring to the spirit of worship, but to a miraculous trance given him by the Holy Spirit, for the purpose of revealing a vision with a message. We learn this by reading Revelation 4:1-2, Revelation 17:3, and Revelation 21:10. The Lord's Day is a reference to the first day of the week, Sunday.

John adds that he heard *a great voice, as of a trumpet.* **1:10** Please note that John did not hear a trumpet, but a loud voice *as* of a trumpet. This figure of speech, called a *simile,* is used often in Revelation to make a comparison. Look for the words *as* and *like,* which introduce similes.

The voice said, *"I am Alpha and the Omega, the first and the last. What you see, write in a book and send it to the seven churches which are in Asia: to Ephesus, and to Smyrna, and to Pergamos, and to Thyatira, and to Sardis, and to Philadelphia, and to Laodicea."* **1:11** These seven churches are listed in the order that a person would take as he carried the book of Revelation from city to city. Beginning with Ephesus, the closest city to the island of Patmos, he would travel in a clockwise circuit. Locate the island of Patmos and these seven cities on a Bible map.

John turned to see the voice that spoke to him, and he saw *seven golden lampstands, and in the midst of the seven lampstands One like the Son of Man.* **1:12-13** NKJV Jesus often referred to himself as "the Son of Man" to emphasize his human nature, as in Matthew 20:28. Daniel described the Christ as "the Son of Man" who would be given "dominion, and glory, and a kingdom." (Daniel 7:13-14) Christ is claiming eternal deity with God the Father in 1:11, by saying, "I am the Alpha and Omega." (cf. 1:8) He is the member of the Godhead that "became flesh and dwelt among us." (John 1:14)

Jesus Christ appears in the first vision of Revelation in a symbolic form. **1:13-16** He is clothed with a garment down to his feet like the robe worn by the High Priest. (Exodus 28:2) Around his chest is a golden band like a king. His head and hair are white as snow signifying the purity of his mind. Having eyes like flaming fire, he searches and judges the lives of men. His feet are like fine bronze enabling him to crush his enemies. His voice as the sound of many waters has power and authority. He has in his right hand seven stars that are the angels or messengers of the seven churches. (1:20) Out of his mouth goes a sharp two-edged sword, which is the word of God. (Hebrews 4:12) And his countenance is like the sun with his face radiating the glory of God. This vision reveals that Jesus is now our prophet, priest, and king as promised in Deuteronomy 18:15-18, Psalm 110:1-4, and Isaiah 9:6-7. Christ has God's word, symbolized by *a sharp two-edged sword*, going out of his mouth. He is the prophet whom we must hear in all things. (Acts 3:22-26) Jesus is now our High Priest that ever lives to make intercession for us. (Hebrews 4:14-16; 7:25) As king, Christ has all power in heaven and on earth. (Matthew 28:18, Acts 2:32-36)

John said, *"When I saw him, I fell at his feet as dead."* But Jesus laid his right hand on John, saying, *"Fear not."* **1:17** Christ is with his church. This vision should comfort and empower Christians. Jesus appears as the Son of Man, but his eternal divine nature is the reason why John should not be afraid. He said, *"I am the first and the last."* **1:17**

"I am he who lives, and was dead, and behold, I am alive forevermore." **1:18** These words reveal **the key to the Revelation.** Jesus **was living** during his earthly ministry of three-and-a-half years. He had oppositions and threats on his life, but he was able to teach and preach. Then, Jesus **was dead** for three days in the tomb.

His enemies thought they had defeated him. The rulers mocked him and rejoiced in his death. But after three days, Jesus was resurrected from the grave and was **the victor** over his enemies. (Romans 1:3-5, Acts 2:32-36)

Jesus was comforting John, who at that time was "in the tribulation." (1:9) After being exiled to the island of Patmos, John received the Revelation in which he was promised, "You must prophesy again." (10:11) Jesus was reminding John that "It is enough for the disciple that he be as his master, and the servant as his lord." (Matthew 10:25) Throughout the book, *he who lives* describes **a long period of evangelism** that is like Christ's ministry of three-and-a-half years. The words *and was dead* describes **a short period of tribulation**. Then comes **the victory;** *I am alive* in a spiritual resurrection. There were ten periods of persecution against the church during the Roman Empire. (page 4) This cycle will be repeated many times before the return of Christ.

In Revelation 11:3-6, the church is symbolized by two witnesses who are able to preach for three-and-a-half years along with opposition. Then the beast comes up out of the bottomless pit and kills the two witnesses. The church appears to be dead for three-and-half days. After this short time, the church comes back to life like the resurrection of Jesus from the dead. (11:7-11)

This pattern is also seen when the seven seals are opened in Revelation 6. When the first seal was opened, Christ, as the Rider on the white horse, goes forth conquering with the gospel being preached by his church. Seals 2 – 4, with red, black, and pale horses, also belong to this period of evangelism. The wars, economic hardships and death, which are symbolized by these horses, cause men to be more receptive to the gospel. When the fifth seal was opened, John saw the souls of martyred saints, representing a period of persecution that lasts for only a little while. (6:9-11) The opening of the sixth seal is victory for the church. The persecutors of the church are punished on the day of the Lord's wrath that is in time. (6:12-17; 16:10-16) The church is able to preach again. The chart on page 211 shows that Revelation 1:18 is the key to understanding the book.

Christ has *the keys of Hades and of death.* **1:18** NKJV Jesus has conquered death; therefore, Christians should not fear it. (1 Cor. 15:54-57) Christ said that the gates of Hades will not be victorious over his church in Matthew 16:18. John was instructed to write about the things which he had seen, and the things which were present, and the things which would take place in the future. **1:19**

In **1:20**, Jesus explains the symbolism of the seven lampstands and the seven stars that were in his right hand. The seven stars are the angels or messengers of the seven churches of Asia to whom the book was originally sent. The seven lampstands represent the seven churches. Jesus says the book is symbolic. You have his word! It is not to be interpreted literally. Too many "prophecy experts" are not listening to Jesus.

Symbolism is one of the literary characteristics of the book of Revelation. The number *seven* is used over fifty times; it stands for perfection and completeness. Most of the symbols are from the Old Testament, especially from the tabernacle and the Exodus. The Most Holy Place was ten cubits wide and ten cubits long and ten cubits high. Ten times ten times ten equal a thousand. Since the presence of God was symbolized by the Most Holy Place, a *thousand* is the symbolic number for heaven.

Parallelism is another literary characteristic of the book. It is *thought rhyme* – not word rhyme, and it is used in Hebrew poetry throughout the Scriptures. Often the second line repeats the thought of the first line using different words. An example is in Psalm 51:2, "Wash me thoroughly from my iniquity, and cleanse me from my sin." The work of the church parallels the ministry of Christ as seen in Revelation 1:18, the key to the book. Also, there are seven parallel views of the victorious church in the book of Revelation.

Seven Views of the Victorious Church

View 1: The Seven Lampstands, Revelation 1 – 3

View 2: The Seven Seals, Revelation 4 – 7

View 3: The Seven Trumpets, Revelation 8 – 11

View 4: The Victorious Lamb, Revelation 12 – 14

View 5: The Seven Bowls of Wrath, Rev. 15 – 16

View 6: The Marriage of the Lamb, Rev. 17 – 19

View 7: The Victorious Church, Revelation 20 – 22

In the last chapter of each view, the end of time has come. You may observe this for yourself by reading Revelation 3:21; Revelation 7:15-17; Revelation 11:18; Revelation 14:7-16; Revelation 16:19-20; Revelation 19:20-21; and Revelation 22:14.

Review Questions on Lesson 1

1. What is the purpose of Revelation? _____
   _____

2. What is the theme of Revelation? _____
   _____

3. The time was "_____" in the first century for the fulfillment of the prophecies in Revelation. 1:3

4. Revelation was written to seven_____ in the Roman province of _____.

5. "The seven Spirits" are the _____ _____.

6. What three things is Jesus called in Rev. 1:5?

   (1) _____
   (2) _____
   (3) _____

7. Sins are washed away by Christ's blood when we are _____ into his death and when we walk in the _____ and _____ our sins.

8. Christ made us to be _____ and _____ unto God. 1:6

9. Who will see Jesus when he comes? _____

10. How does God describe himself in Rev. 1:8?
    _____

11. John was a companion with first century Christians in the _____ and in the _____ and the _____ of Jesus Christ. 1:9

12. John was on the island of _____ for the word of _____ and for the _____ of Jesus Christ. 1:9

13. John saw seven golden _____, and in their midst was _____.

14. Christ said to John "_____." 1:17

15. What verse is the key to Revelation? _____

16. There were _____ periods of severe persecution by the Romans against the church.

17. The seven lampstands are the seven _____ in the Roman province of _____.

18. What are the seven stars in Christ's right hand? 1:20
    _____

19. Two Hebrew literary characteristics in the book are _____ and _____.

20. Revelation reveals _____ parallel views of the church.

21. The end of _____ has come at the end of each view.

Letters to the Seven Churches
Revelation 2 – 3

In the first vision, John saw Jesus Christ walking among seven lampstands representing seven churches in the Roman province of Asia. We are reminded of the words of Jesus in Matthew 28:20, "And lo, I am with you always." Now Jesus instructs John to write a letter to each congregation.

Each letter is addressed **to the angel** of the church. Our English word "angel" is a transliteration of the Greek word meaning **messenger**. There are earthly messengers as well as heavenly ones. This same Greek word is used to describe John the Baptist as an earthly messenger in Mark 1:2. The messenger of the church would be the one who would read the letter to the congregation. (Rev. 1:3)

In the introduction of each letter, Jesus uses symbols from the first vision in chapter one to describe himself. His self-descriptions fit the special needs of each congregation. Jesus knows the "works" of the churches. He begins each letter with praise whenever possible followed by rebuke and correction when needed. The only churches without reproof are Smyrna and Philadelphia. Laodicea is without any praise; it receives only condemnation.

Jesus wants all Christians to benefit from the letters written to these seven churches. The Lord had more than seven churches in the province of Asia. Congregations were also at Troas, Colosse, and Hierapolis.[18] Why were the letters limited to seven churches? Hendriksen gives the following answer, "Seven is the number which

---

[18] Acts 20:6-7 and Colossians 1:2; 4:12-13

symbolizes completeness. It clearly indicates that the admonitions and consolations of this book were meant for the entire church throughout the centuries."[19] Each letter concludes with a promise made to the individual who overcomes, along with this admonition, "He that has an ear, let him hear what the Spirit says unto the churches."

Ephesus – Left Its First Love

Ephesus was the greatest city in the Roman province of Asia. The city was located on the Cayster River near the Aegean Sea. It was the home of one of the seven wonders of the ancient world—the temple of Artemis (or Diana, KJV). Paul was in Ephesus for three years during his third journey. (Acts 20:17-31) As a result of his teaching in the school of Tyrannus, the entire province of Asia heard the word of the Lord. (Acts 19:9-10) Later, we find Timothy working with this church. (1 Tim. 1:3) From church history we learn that John was in Ephesus before and after his exile on Patmos.

"These things says He who holds the seven stars in His right hand, who walks in the midst of the seven golden lampstands." 2:1 NKJV Those in Ephesus needed to be reminded of Christ's presence and their dependence upon him. He is supporting the seven stars—messengers or preachers that proclaim his word. Christ is with his church.

Jesus praises the church in Ephesus for their good works, their perseverance, and their strong stand against false apostles. **2:2-3** They had heeded Paul's warning concerning false teachers. (Acts 20:29-31) ***"Nevertheless I have somewhat against you, because you have left your first love." 2:4*** Without love for God and others, we fail to obey the greatest commandments. (Matt. 22:34-40)

---

[19] W. Hendriksen, *More Than Conquerors*, p. 15

Without love, our preaching and teaching is just so much noise, and our hard work and sacrifices are for nothing. (1 Cor. 13:1-3) We must not only guard against the danger of false teachers but also against the danger of our being lifted up in pride as we condemn their false teaching. In our stand for truth, let us not forget God and our dependence upon him. This was the sin of the Pharisees. (Matt. 23:23)

"Remember therefore from where you are fallen, and repent and do the first works." 2:5 The fallen Christian must repent and pray to be forgiven. (Acts 8:22, 1 John 1:9) Christ warns the church at Ephesus that he would come quickly and remove their lampstand from its place if they did not repent. Jesus was giving them time to repent. However, if they would not repent, they would cease being his church. Not every church that calls itself a "church of Christ" is his church.

"But this you have, that you hate the deeds of the Nicolaitans, which I also hate." 2:6 Jesus did not want them to conclude that restoring love meant that they should go soft on exposing false doctrine and ungodly living. He praises them for hating the deeds of the Nicolaitans. While Jesus condemns them for leaving their first love, he is not condemning their strong stand against false teaching. Christian love does not exclude our speaking out against wickedness and religious error. There are some things we must hate. We are to "hate the evil, and love the good." (Amos 5:15) Jesus himself hated the practices of the Nicolaitans, a gnostic group that ate foods sacrificed to idols and engaged in immoral practices. (Rev. 2:14-15)

Christ concludes the letter to Ephesus with this promise: *"To him that overcomes, will I give to eat of the tree of life, which is in the midst of the paradise of God." 2:7* The church at Ephesus is reminded that our spiritual life depends upon our fellowship with God. (1 John 1:3-7) The tree of life is in the heavenly city, the New Jerusalem in Revelation 22:2.

Smyrna – Poor, But Rich Spiritually

The city of Smyrna (modern Izmir, Turkey) is forty miles north of Ephesus. With an excellent harbor, the city became a center of commerce. Because of its loyalty to Rome, Smyrna was the first city in the province of Asia to erect a temple to the goddess Roma in 195 BC. The city became a center for the worship of Roman emperors. It was one of the most beautiful cities of the world in the first century. Smyrna is the birthplace of Homer, the famous Greek poet.[20]

*"These things says the first and the last, which was dead, and is alive; I know your works and tribulation and poverty, but you are rich." * **2:8-9** Christians in Smyrna were to be comforted in the knowledge that their eternal Lord had conquered death. They should not fear nor be defeated by the things they were suffering. They were living in a city of wealth, but they were in economic poverty. Yet they were rich! They were enjoying all spiritual blessings in Christ, and they had an eternal inheritance in heaven. For the faithful church in Smyrna, the Lord had no condemnation.

*"I know the blasphemy of them which say they are Jews, and are not, but are the synagogue of Satan." * **2:9** Jesus told the Jews who were rejecting him that their father was the devil, even though they were Abraham's descendants. (John 8:37-45) Any Jew who has not received the spiritual circumcision performed by God by being buried with Christ in baptism and raised with him through faith is not a true Jew. (Romans 2:28, Colossians

---

[20] J. T. Marlin, *The Seven Churches of Asia*, pp. 51-53

2:11-12) Today, Christians are the chosen people of God and his holy nation. (1 Peter 2:9) Just as the unbelieving Jews falsely accused Jesus, they were slandering his disciples in Smyrna.

The church is not to fear the things they were about to suffer, because they would have *tribulation ten days.* Jesus promises, *"Be faithful unto death, and I will give you a crown of life."* **2:10** The devil is behind all the tribulations that Christians face. (Ephesians 6:12) The **ten days** refer to the ten periods of persecution during the time of the Roman Empire. (Rev. 17:12-14) Polycarp, an elder in the church at Smyrna, was executed during the fourth period of persecution. He courageously faced his death by saying, "You threaten with the fire that burns for a time, and is quickly quenched, for you do not know the fire that awaits the wicked in the judgment to come and in everlasting punishment."[21] Polycarp was faithful even to the point of death, because he trusted Jesus who had promised to give him a crown of life. Paul also spoke of this crown as he faced death by Nero, during the first Roman persecution of Christians. (2 Timothy 4:6-8)

"He that overcomes shall not be hurt by the second death." **2:11** Hell is described in Revelation 20:14 as "the lake of fire" and "the second death."

Pergamos – Tolerated the Doctrine of Balaam

The city of Pergamos was built on a hill with the Aegean Sea in view fifteen miles away. It was the farthest north of the seven churches of Asia. The city was famous for its great library and its invention of parchment as a writing material.

---

[21] Paul Maier, *Eusebius—The Church History*, p. 150

Christ has ***the sharp sword with two edges. 2:12*** The word of God is described as being "sharper than any two-edged sword" in Hebrews 4:12. The church at Pergamos was tolerating false teaching that Christ will rebuke with God's word.

Satan's seat or throne was in Pergamos. **2:13** This is a reference either to their great altar to Zeus, high on the hill of Pergamos, or more likely to the temple dedicated to the worship of the Roman emperors. In the midst of these idolatrous influences, most of the congregation had held fast to the name and faith of Christ even while they were being persecuted; and one of them named Antipas was killed as a faithful martyr. They are praised for their firm stand in faith.

However, Jesus criticizes the church at Pergamos for tolerating those who held ***the doctrine of Balaam. 2:14*** At the time of the Exodus, a prophet of God from Pethor of Mesopotamia named Balaam was hired by Balak king of Moab to curse Israel. (Num. 22:1 – 25:9) When God turned Balaam's words into blessings, the prophet advised Balak to tempt the men of Israel with sexual immorality and with the worship of their gods. God then cursed Israel with a plague that killed 24,000. (Numbers 31:13-16) Balaam became a symbol for all who do not love the truth but desire the wages of unrighteousness. (2 Peter 2:15; Jude 11) Within the church at Pergamos, some were teaching a false doctrine leading to sinful conduct. Most of its members were not guilty of eating foods sacrificed to idols or practicing sexual immorality, but they were tolerating those who did these things. ***"So you also have them that hold the doctrine of the Nicolaitans, which thing I hate." 2:15*** Like Ephesus, Pergamos "also" had Nicolaitans among them. The teaching of the Nicolaitans was like that of Balaam who promoted laxity among God's people. Their love of money led them to offer incense to the Roman emperors and eat foods sacrificed to idols so they could buy and sell in the marketplace. (Rev. 13:17) To be socially accepted some even engaged in the sexual immorality of the pagans. While the Lord praised the church in Ephesus for hating the practices of the Nicolaitans, he condemned the church in Pergamos for tolerating them. Christians are to "have no fellowship with the unfruitful works of darkness, but rather reprove them." (Eph. 5:11)

Christ commands the church, **"Repent, or else I will come unto you quickly and fight against them with the sword of my mouth." 2:16** God's word is the weapon that he uses to destroy all false teachings, thoughts, and practices. (2 Cor. 10:3-6, Ephesians 6:17, Rev. 1:16)

"He that has an ear, let him hear what the Spirit says unto the churches." 2:17 Today, some compromise the truth so they can be accepted by the "in" crowd and get ahead economically. Listen to the Spirit!

Jesus promises to the person who overcomes: **"I will give to eat of the hidden manna, and give him a white stone, and in the stone a new name written, which no man knows saving he that receives it." 2:17** The Lord will provide for the faithful just as he sustained Israel in the wilderness with manna from heaven. Jesus is the true bread from heaven; his words are spirit, and they are life. (John 6:30-35, 63) A white stone was the stone of acquittal in trials. It also may be thought of as a ticket to a banquet with one's special name on it. (Rev. 19:9) The new name may be referring to the name Christian. (Isaiah 62:2 and Acts 11:18, 26)

Thyatira – Tolerated Jezebel

Thyatira was located forty miles southeast of Pergamos. The first three churches were on or near the coast, while the last four were some distance inland.

Thyatira, being situated in a valley connecting two other valleys, became a commercial center. Although the city was not nearly as large as Ephesus, Smyrna, and Pergamos, it had the most highly organized trade guilds in the ancient world. Among these trade unions were the bronze workers, potters, tanners, and garment makers. Thyatira was famous for its purple dye. Paul's first convert in Philippi was Lydia, a seller of purple from the city of Thyatira. (Acts 16:13-14) Since there was no temple to the Roman emperors in the city, the church was not threatened with severe persecution as in the three previous cities. Their temptations came from the trade guilds; each guild had its own god. If you wanted to be involved in society and get the best paying jobs, you had to join a trade union. "The monthly meetings were characterized by eating meats sacrificed to idols and drinking alcoholic beverages. Sexual immorality was also a part of the guild system."[22] A faithful Christian could not belong to a trade guild.

Jesus describes himself as *"the Son of God, who has eyes like a flame of fire."* **2:18** The Son of man in the first vision is plainly identified here as "the Son of God." With penetrating eyes, he sees and judges; he is the one who **searches** the hearts of men. (2:23) Thyatira was known for its bronze, but Jesus with his feet like fine bronze is far superior. The armor of God includes having "your feet shod with the preparation of the gospel of peace." (Ephesians 6:15) The gospel of Christ is more enduring than the teachings of men.

Jesus said, *"I know your deeds, your love and faith, your service and perseverance, and that you are now doing more than you did at first."* **2:19** [NIV] They had the love that the church in Ephesus was lacking. They were showing their faith by their caring service, steadfastness,

---

[22] Joe D. Jones, *Victory in Jesus*, p. 54

and continued growth. If the letter had ended here, the church in Thyatira would be remembered as a great congregation. But such is not the case.

You suffer that woman Jezebel, which calls herself a prophetess, to teach and to seduce my servants to commit fornication and eat things sacrificed unto idols. **2:20** Their fault was the same as that at Pergamos. They were tolerating false teaching. Some of their members were being led into sin. Again, reference is made to an Old Testament character. Pergamos had its Balaam; Thyatira had its Jezebel. This name is symbolic— no one would name a daughter after the wicked Jezebel, who led God's people into the worship of idols and sexual immorality. (1 Kings 16:30-33; 21:25) Since a woman in Revelation 12 symbolizes the church, Jezebel may be symbolizing an apostate group within the church at Thyatira. She was claiming to be receiving special messages from God. She was assuring Christians that they could attend the trade guild meetings and take part in their activities without sinning; in fact it is good to know *"the depths of Satan."* **2.24** Christ gave her time to repent. **2:21** If the Jezebel group would not repent, she would be punished with suffering and death. **2:22-23** Peter tells us, "The Lord is not slack concerning his promise, as some men count slackness, but is longsuffering to us, not willing that any should perish, but that all should come to repentance." (2 Peter 3:9) Jesus says, *"I am he who searches the minds and hearts. And I will give to each one of you according to your works."* **2:23** NKJV

"And he that overcomes, and keeps my works unto the end, to him will I give power over the nations." **2:26** The Christian has power because he is with Christ, who has all power and authority in heaven and on earth. (Matthew 28:18-20, Hebrews 13:5-6)

"He shall rule them with a rod of iron." 2:27 This a quotation from Psalm 2:9 and is a reference to the rule of Christ. The victory is with Christ the King. The faithful Christian is also promised *"the morning star." 2:28* Jesus Christ is the Morning Star in Revelation 22:16.

Sardis – Was Dead

Sardis was in the center of the Roman province of Asia—thirty miles south-southeast of Thyatira. It was built on a high hill with cliffs on three sides that were thought to be inaccessible. Sardis was once the capital of the wealthy kingdom of Lydia, which was famous for making the world's first coins for money, over six hundred years before Christ. In the first century, the people of Sardis "worshiped Cybele in a frenzied and hysterical way rather than the Emperor."[23] She was worshiped as the nature goddess, who gives life.

Christ has *"the seven Spirits of God and the seven stars." 3:1* The Holy Spirit is the seven Spirits. (1:4) Jesus said, "The words that I speak unto you, they are spirit, and they are life." (John 6:63) Jesus sent the Holy Spirit to his apostles to guide them into all truth. (John 14:26, John 16:12-15) The mystery has been revealed by the Holy Spirit to God's holy apostles and prophets. (Eph. 3:4) Peter said, "His divine power has given unto us all things that pertain unto life and godliness." (2 Pet. 1:3) Christ holds the seven stars, his preachers, in his right hand while they proclaim his gospel given by the Holy Spirit. (Rev. 1:20)

Jesus said to those in Sardis, *"You have a reputation of being alive, but you are dead." 3:1* NIV Some have suggested that the sin of the church was the condition of their city—living on their past reputation. However, Jesus

---

[23] J. T. Marlin, *The Seven Churches of Asia Minor*, p. 107

said that they, at that time, had a reputation of being alive. Their numbers were growing! But most of them had defiled themselves with false teaching and sinful living. Perhaps they thought they had to compete with the exciting worship of Cybele. No doubt their worship services were very lively and entertaining, but they were not worshiping God "in spirit and in truth." (John 4:24) In their zeal to grow a large church, they had forgotten the source of their life—Jesus Christ. "God has given to us eternal life, and this life is in his Son. He that has the Son has life, and he that has not the Son of God has not life." (1 John 5:11-12) They were dead, because they did not have Jesus!

The Lord had not completely given up on the church in Sardis. He encouraged the faithful few to *be watchful and strengthen the things which remain, that are ready to die.* **3:2** Some life was remaining in the church, but the faithful members should be aware of those that were leading the church astray. Only by returning to Jesus, the source of life, could the church be strong and alive. *"Remember therefore how you have received and heard, and hold fast and repent."* **3:3** They were in a similar condition as the churches in Galatia years earlier when Paul warned them: "I marvel that you are so soon removed from him that called you into the grace of Christ unto another gospel: which is not another; but there are some that trouble you, and would pervert the gospel of Christ." (Galatians 1:6-7) Repent or perish!

Christ warned, *"I will come on you as a thief, and you shall not know what hour I will come upon you."* **3:3** God pours out six bowls of wrath upon sinners before the Day of Judgment, the seventh bowl. (Rev. 15-16) His coming would be "as a thief" — unannounced and unexpected. Twice in their history, the city of Sardis had been taken by surprise. In the sixth century BC, some soldiers of Cyrus king of Persia scaled the high cliffs in the night and defeated them. Later the army of a Seleucid king did the same thing. A sudden earthquake destroyed the city in AD 17.[24]

Although the church as a whole was dead, Jesus said, ***"You have a few names even in Sardis which have not defiled their garments; and they shall walk with me in white." 3:4*** They were "the things which remain" that needed to be strengthened. (3:2) The faithful few needed courage to speak the truth in love and bring about a revival to this dead church. They were walking in white garments, because they were walking with Christ, whose blood cleanses us from all sin. (1 John 1:7-10) This letter does not begin with any praise because Sardis was dead.

"He that overcomes, the same shall be clothed in white raiment; and I will not blot out his name out of the book of life, but I will confess his name before my Father, and before his angels." 3:5 What is implied? If a Christian does not overcome, his name will be blotted out of the Book of Life! In his letter to Sardis, Jesus refutes the false doctrine of once saved, always saved! Christ will confess those who confess him. (Matt. 10:32)

Philadelphia – Had an Open Door

The city of Philadelphia was located twenty-eight miles southeast of Sardis; it was one of the newer cities of Asia. King Attalus II Philadelphus built it in the second century BC for the purpose of spreading the Greek culture.[25] It was called "Little Athens" because of its beautiful temples and public buildings. Philadelphia was famous for its wine, and its coins bore the image of Bacchus the god of wine.[26]

---

[24] J. T. Marlin, *The Seven Churches of Asia Minor*, pp. 110-11

[25] Joe D. Jones, *Victory in Jesus*, p. 64

[26] J. T. Marlin, *The Seven Churches of Asia Minor*, pp. 122-123

Christ describes himself as *"he that is holy, he that is true, he that has the key of David, he that opens and no man shuts, and shuts and no man opens."* **3:7** We are made holy in Christ, who is holy. (Eph. 5:25-27) Jesus is true, and he makes us a part of his church, the true temple of God. (Eph. 2:19-22) The key of David is referring to Isaiah 22:20-22. During Hezekiah's reign as king of Judah, Eliakim became the steward of the king's palace and was given the key of David to open and shut the doors of the palace. In a time of tribulation, he was confronted by the messengers of the king of Assyria, Sennacherib, who had shut up Jerusalem with his armies. (2 Kings 18:18, 26) However, Eliakim was able to open the gates of Jerusalem again when, in fulfillment of Isaiah's prophecy, God destroyed one hundred and eighty-five thousand men in the camp of the Assyrians at night. (2 Kings 19:1-7, 35-37) With the key of David, Jesus opens heaven's gates to the faithful and shuts out the wicked. (Rev. 22:14-15)

Because the church in Philadelphia had kept his word and had not denied his name, Christ calls upon them to see with the eye of faith what he has in store for them. *"Behold, I have set before you an open door, and no one can shut it."* **3:8** In the next chapter, John sees "a door standing open in heaven." (4:1) The Christian had excluded himself from the temples and the social life of the pagans. The unbelieving Jews had put him out of their synagogues. (John 9:22) But for him, a door is open in heaven! It is the entrance into the everlasting kingdom. (2 Peter 1:11) The church was relatively few in numbers and lacking in material wealth. They had *little strength* physically, but they were strong spiritually in the Lord. (Ephesians 6:10)

"Behold, I will make them of the synagogue of Satan, which say they are Jews, and are not, but do lie; behold, I will make them come and worship before your

feet, and to know that I have loved you." **3:9** Twice now Jesus has stated plainly that the Jews are no longer God's special people. If they reject Jesus, they belong to Satan. (Rev. 2:9) Jesus exposes the error of any interpretation of prophecy that makes physical Israel the object of God's special blessings. Jesus assures his faithful church they will be victorious over their Jewish persecutors.

Christ would keep his faithful saints from *"the hour of trial that is going to come upon the whole world to test those who live on the earth."* **3:10** ᴺᴷᴶⱽ Jesus has nothing but praise for the church in Philadelphia, because they had endured patiently various trials. The description *"those who live on the earth"* designates those who are opposed to Christ and his church. (Read Revelation 6:10, 8:13, 11:10, 13:8, 13:14, and 17:8.) When the trumpets sound and the bowls of wrath are poured out, the church would have nothing to fear.

"Behold, I come quickly; hold that fast which you have, that no man take your crown." **3:11** Jesus is coming suddenly! He warns us of the possibility of being lost after being saved. If it is not possible to lose your crown, why did Jesus give this warning?

To the one who overcomes, Christ promises, *"I will make a pillar in the temple of my God ... and I will write upon him the name of my God, and the name of the city of my God, which is New Jerusalem ... and I will write upon him my new name."* **3:12** The faithful Christian will be part of God's temple in heaven forever. As a child of God, he will have his Father's name. He also will have the name of the New Jerusalem with the blessings of citizenship in the heavenly city. (Rev. 21) Christ's new name "Son" is given to him that overcomes. (Hebrews 1:1-5) "He that overcomes shall inherit all things; and I will be his God and he shall be my son." (Rev. 21:7)

Laodicea – Was Lukewarm

The city of Laodicea was located about forty miles southeast of Philadelphia and east of Ephesus. Epaphras appears to have planted the church in Laodicea and in the nearby cities of Colosse and Hierapolis. (Col. 4:12-13; 1:7) Laodicea had a medical school that specialized in the treatment of sore eyes, and it was well known for its eye salve. The Laodiceans were also famous for their clothing made of black wool. Located at the crossing of three great highways, Laodicea became a great commercial and financial center. When an earthquake destroyed their city in AD 60, they rejected Roman aid and rebuilt it at their own expense. The city appears not to have been involved in emperor worship; its god was wealth. The church had the attitudes of this wealthy independent city.

Christ describes himself as *"the Amen, the faithful and true witness, the beginning of the creation of God."* **3:14** The word *amen* verifies that what has been said is true. By his resurrection from the dead, Jesus proved his claims. (Romans 1:4, John 2:18-22) As the faithful and true witness, he will tell the truth about the spiritual condition of his people. Jesus Christ is the source of God's physical creation because he created all things. (Col. 1:16-18) He is also the beginning of God's spiritual creation, the church.

Jesus testifies: *"I know your works, that you are neither cold nor hot. I would that you were cold or hot. So then because you are lukewarm, neither cold nor hot, I will spew you out of my mouth."* **3:15, 16** Stafford North observes, "Cold water has value and so does hot water, but lukewarm is useless."[27] Laodicea was located on the Lycus River, which flows from the east to west

---

[27] Stafford North, *Unlocking Revelation*, p. 38

and into the Maeander River. Ten miles east of Laodicea was the city of Colosse at the foot of snowcapped Mount Cadmus with streams of refreshing cold water flowing into the Lycus River. Six miles to the northeast of Laodicea was Hierapolis with its hot springs for comforting and healing baths. This hot water entered the cold water of the Lycus River just east of Laodicea, producing lukewarm water that was nauseating. The church at Laodicea is the only church for which the Lord had no praise! They did not have any terrible sinners among them—no Balaams or Jezebels, but they were not zealous for the Lord and his work. They were useless, proud, and indifferent! This lukewarm spiritual condition was nauseating to Jesus.

The church was saying, **"I am rich, and increased with goods, and have need of nothing."** But they did not know that they were **"wretched, and miserable and poor, and blind, and naked." 3:17** In their pride, they had deceived themselves. They were financially rich, but poor spiritually. They were the opposite of the church in Smyrna, the poor rich church. Jesus is the true witness of our condition today.

Jesus says, **"I counsel you to buy of me gold tried in the fire, that you may be rich."** As gold is refined by fire, a genuine faith in Jesus is tested by trials and is rewarded with true riches. (1 Peter 1:6-9) **"And white garments, that you may be clothed."** They needed to be clothed with Christ and his righteousness. (Galatians 3:27 and 1 Corinthians 1:30) In contrast to their black woolen clothing, they needed a robe made white in the blood of the Lamb. (Rev. 7:9-10) **"And anoint your eyes with eye salve, that you may see." 3:18** This is a reference to their successful medical school. Only Jesus can give spiritual sight when our eyes are focused on him. (Eph. 4:17-21, Heb. 12:2) They could buy these things from Jesus without money. (Isaiah 55:1-3) Salvation is free!

However, there is the cost of self-denial. (Luke 9:23-24, Luke 14:27-33) Jesus rebuked the Laodiceans with blunt words of correction because he loves them. *"As many as I love, I rebuke and chasten: be zealous there-fore, and repent."* **3:19**

"Behold, I stand at the door and knock: if any man hears my voice and opens the door, I will come in to him and will sup with him, and he with me." **3:20** Their self-sufficiency and indifference toward God had forced Jesus out of their lives. He pictures himself as standing outside the door of their heart, knocking, hoping that they will invite him in and have fellowship with him again. God will not force his way into our hearts. We must invite him in.

Christ promises, *"To him that overcomes will I grant to sit with me in my throne, even as I also overcame and am set down with my Father in his throne."* **3:21** Jesus is promising fellowship with him in the most exalted position possible. In him we have the victorious life.

"He that has an ear, let him hear what the Spirit says to the churches." **3:22** We may find ourselves in similar circumstances as these seven churches. Today, as then, not all churches of Christ are what they should be. All but two of these seven churches had serious faults that needed to be corrected. We are to be faithful even if our congregation is lukewarm, tolerating sin and false doctrine, and/or lacking love. We are reminded that we will be judged as individuals. The message of Revelation is not just for Christians living during the days of the Roman Empire. If you have an ear, you are to hear what the Spirit says to the churches. These inspired words will correct, instruct, encourage, and comfort you.

Seven Lessons from the Seven Letters

1. In exposing error, we must guard against losing our love for God and our dependence upon him. (2:4)

2. Ephesus and the "Jezebel" group at Thyatira were given "time to repent." (2:5 and 2:21)

3. Unbelieving Jews are "the synagogue of Satan." (2:9 and 3:9)

4. Ten periods of persecution by the Romans against the church were predicted in Revelation 2:10.

5. Loving churches should not tolerate sinful members like Pergamos and Thyatira did. (2:14 and 2:20)

6. If we are not faithful, our name will be blotted out of the Book of Life, and we will lose our crown. (3:5 and 3:11)

7. Christ states, "As many as I love, I rebuke and chasten: be zealous therefore and repent. Behold, I stand at the door and knock; if any man hear my voice, and open the door, I will come in to him." (3:19-20)

Review Questions on Lesson 2

1. The word *angel* means _____.

2. Jesus began each letter with _____ if possible.

3. Jesus said, "I know your _____."

4. The church at Ephesus had left its first _____.

5. What praise did Jesus have for the church at Ephesus?
   _____
   _____

6. Jesus hated the deeds of the _____.

7. What would Jesus do if the church at Ephesus did not repent? _____

8. He who _____ will eat from the tree of life.

9. Smyrna was _____ economically, but the church was _____ spiritually.

10. Jesus said the synagogue of the Jews was the synagogue of _____. 2:9

11. Christians would have tribulation for _____ days.

12. The faithful will be given "a _____ of life."

13. Pergamos was tolerating the doctrine of _____.

14. Pergamos also had those that held the teachings of the _____ as did Ephesus.

15. Thyatira tolerated a _____.

16. The church at Thyatira had _____ that was lacking in Ephesus.

17. The Jezebel group was given time to _____.

18. Sardis had a reputation of being _____, but was _____.

19. Jesus said that a person's name could be blotted out of the book of _____. 3:5

20. Those at Philadelphia had an _____ _____.

21. There is an open door in _____ for the faithful. 4:1

22. In 3:11 Jesus said we could lose our _____.

23. The church at Laodicea was _____.

24. Whom does the Lord rebuke and chasten, according to 3:19? _____

25. The Lord knocks wanting us to _____ the door. 3:20

26. The church at _____ did not receive any praise.

27. The two churches receiving no condemnation were at _____ and _____.

View 2

The Seven Seals

Revelation 4 – 7

NOTES

The Open Door in Heaven
Revelation 4 – 5

After the first vision that included the letters to the seven churches, John saw a second vision. He saw *a door standing open in heaven.* **4:1** John heard again the voice of Christ, the one that sounded like a trumpet in 1:10. The Lord invited John to come up to him for the purpose of revealing future things. This is the beginning of the second view of the victorious church.

John was immediately in the Spirit; and, *behold, a throne was set in heaven, and one sat on the throne.* **4:2** Being "in the Spirit" made it possible for John to go up and enter the open door in the vision. He was able to see God on his throne. John saw a symbolic representation of heaven—not the real place. Later in this vision, John will see the Lamb that has redeemed us by his blood. (5:6) Our redemption is by the blood of Jesus Christ. (Eph. 1:7) In heaven, we will not see a literal lamb with seven horns and seven eyes, but we will see Jesus. The purpose of this vision is to show us, in beautiful symbolism, that God rules the earth and the universe from his throne in heaven. He is in control of all things. "And we know that God causes all things to work together for good to those who love God, to those who are called according to His purpose." (Romans 8:28) ^{NASB}

Three symbols are used to describe God the Father, who sits on the throne in heaven. **4:3** The first is a *jasper* stone that is said to be "clear as crystal" in Revelation 21:11. God's holiness is like a crystal clear, sparking diamond. The second symbol is the *sardius* stone, a transliteration of the original Greek word which refers to the carnelian. This red stone represents God's wrath and justice. The third symbol is the *emerald rainbow* around the throne, reminding us of God's mercy following the flood. (Genesis 9:11-16) When faced with various trials, let's always remember our holy, just and merciful God, who is on the throne in heaven.

And round about the throne were twenty-four seats, and upon the seats I saw twenty-four elders sitting, clothed in white raiment; and they had on their heads crowns of gold. **4:4** The twenty-four elders represent the faithful leaders of the twelve tribes of Israel and the twelve apostles of the new covenant. This interpretation is supported by Revelation 21:12-14, where the names of the twelve tribes of Israel are on the twelve gates of the New Jerusalem and the names of the twelve apostles are on the twelve foundations of the city. These elders are dressed in white indicating their purity. The golden crowns on their heads are victors' wreaths. The Greek word is *stephanos*, a wreath conferred on a victor.

And out of the throne proceeded lightning and thundering and voices. **4:5** The symbolism around the throne is from the book of Exodus and the Tabernacle. When the Lord came down upon Mount Sinai[28] and spoke the Ten Commandments to Israel, there were flashes of lightning and loud thunder and a voice that caused the people to tremble.[29]

And there were seven lamps of fire burning before the throne, which are the seven Spirits of God. **4:5** In the Holy Place of the Tabernacle, seven lamps were burning before the Most Holy Place, which represented the presence of God.[30] The seven lamps are described as "the seven Spirits of God." From Revelation 1:4-5, we conclude that the seven Spirits symbolize the Holy Spirit.

---

[28] Exodus 19:16-20
[29] Exodus 20:1-19
[30] Hebrews 9:1-3, Exodus 25:37, Exodus 40:24-25

The Holy Spirit gives light through his word to show us how to serve God.[31] The Father is on the throne. The Holy Spirit is before the throne. Christ the Lamb is in the midst of the throne. (5:6)

And before the throne there was a sea of glass, like unto crystal. **4:6** This sea of glass was like the laver, the basin of water, before the tabernacle. It was for the washing of the priests before they entered the Holy Place.[32] The sea of glass was like crystal, indicating purity and holiness. The washing corresponds to baptism for us today.[33]

And in the midst of the throne, and around the throne, were four living creatures. **4:6** NKJV "Living creatures" is a better translation than "beasts" as in the KJV. The Greek word is *zoa,* which means living beings. Thayer says that this word is "fitly rendered *living creatures* in contradistinction to the *therion* beast" in Revelation 11:7 and 13:1.[34]

The first living creature was like ***a lion***, the second was like ***a calf***, the third had the face as ***a man***, and the fourth was like ***a flying eagle***. Each living creature had six wings and was full of eyes all around. And they were saying: ***"Holy, holy, holy, Lord God Almighty, which was, and is, and is to come!"*** **4:7-8** Similar living creatures are described in Ezekiel 1:5-10 and are identified as cherubim in Ezekiel 10:19-20. We conclude that they are angels of the highest order. These angels have great power like the lion; they serve like a calf or ox, they possess superior intelligence like a man, and they are swift as an eagle. Their ability to see all things is symbolized by their being "full of eyes." Cherubim were

---

[31] Psalm 119:105, 1 Corinthians 2:9-13
[32] Exodus 30:18-21
[33] Acts 22:16, Galatians 3:27
[34] Joseph H. Thayer, *Greek-English Lexicon of the New Testament*

connected with the Most Holy Place in the Tabernacle. Two cherubim of gold covered the mercy seat facing each other in the Most Holy Place.[35] The veil that separated the Most Holy Place from the Holy Place had "an artistic design of cherubim."[36] In contrast with the lifeless cherubim of the Tabernacle, the four living creatures around the throne can praise God continually. Their praise of "Holy, Holy, Holy, Lord God Almighty" supports the doctrine of the Trinity. God is most holy!

When these four great angels, **the living creatures, give glory and honor and thanks** to God, the twenty-four elders fall down and worship the one who lives forever. They cast their crowns of victory before his throne and praise him for creating all things. **4:9-11** This vision should be a reminder to all Christians who are suffering trials and persecutions that their God is able to give them the ultimate victory in heaven.

John saw in the right hand of God the Father ***a book written within and on the backside, sealed with seven seals.*** **5:1** The Greek word for "book" may also be translated *scroll* as it is in most versions of the Bible. The scroll in the heavenly Father's hand is sealed, indicating future events that have not been revealed. The seven seals symbolize the completeness of the revelation that would be made known when the seals were opened.

Then John saw a strong angel proclaiming with a loud voice, ***"Who is worthy to open the book, and to loose the seals?"*** **5:2-4** John wept because it seemed that no one in the whole universe was qualified to open the scroll that would reveal God's plan for the future.

---

[35] Exodus 37:7-9
[36] Exodus 36:35, NKJV

But one of the elders said to John, ***"Weep not: behold, the Lion of the tribe of Judah, the Root of David, has prevailed to open the book, and to loose the seven seals." 5:5*** The lion, as the king of the forest, symbolizes royalty and courage.[37] A sculptured lion was on each side of the six steps leading up to the throne of King Solomon, and a sculptured lion was beside each armrest of the throne. (1 Kings 10:19-20) Like a lion, the tribe of Judah has "the scepter." (Gen. 49:9-10) Our Lord Jesus is from the kingly tribe of Judah. (Hebrews 7:14) Christ is ***"The Root of David"*** – the descendant of David, who was the first king in this royal lineage. (Isa. 11:1-10) The only one in the entire universe who is able to open the scroll is our Lord Jesus Christ.

In the midst of the throne…stood a Lamb as it had been slain, having seven horns and seven eyes, which are the seven Spirits of God sent forth into all the earth. 5:6 Before Jesus could become the Lion of the tribe of Judah, he had to be "the Lamb of God, which takes away the sin of the world." (John 1:29) The Lamb had been slain, symbolizing the death of Jesus. But John saw the Lamb standing — he had been raised from the dead! Jesus Christ our Lord was "declared to be the Son of God with power, according to the spirit of holiness, by the resurrection from the dead." (Romans 1:4) It was by his death and resurrection, he was qualified to loose the seven seals and reveal God's eternal plan. When used figuratively, ***horns*** represent power and authority.[38] The Lamb has ***seven horns***, showing that Jesus Christ has all power and authority. (Matthew 28:18) His ***seven eyes*** are symbolizing "the seven Spirits of God", the Holy Spirit. (Rev. 1:4) With the Spirit's help, Jesus is able to see all things. (Zech. 3:9, 4:10) He overcame Satan's power and is now on his Father's throne in heaven.

---

[37] *Nelson's Bible Dictionary*, Animals/Lion
[38] Walter Bauer, William F. Arndt, F. Wilber Gingrich, *A Greek-English Lexicon of the New Testament*, 1957 edition, p. 430

When the Lamb had taken the scroll, the four living creatures and the twenty-four elders fell down and worshiped him. Each one of the elders had ***a harp, and golden bowls full of incense, which are the prayers of the saints.* 5:7-8** ^{NKJV} Since the golden bowls of incense are the prayers of the saints, the harp is also symbolic, representing praise to the Lord. We must remember that we are seeing a symbolic view of heaven, not the real place. In heaven we will see cherubim—not four living creatures full of eyes. If musical instruments in worship are authorized because harps are in Revelation, then the use of incense and the offering of animal sacrifices are also authorized in Christian worship. John saw a lamb that had been slain. If harps will be in heaven, then we will not see Jesus in heaven. Instead, we will see a lamb with seven horns and seven eyes. The lamb, and the harp, and the incense are all symbolic.

And the elders ***sung a new song, saying: "You are worthy to take the book, and to open the seals thereof: for you were slain, and have redeemed us to God by your blood." 5:9*** They were singing a new song of redemption. Animal blood was sprinkled on the Mercy Seat that covered the Ark of the Covenant in the Most Holy Place on the Day of Atonement. (Lev. 16:11-15) The slain Lamb, Jesus Christ, is in the midst of the throne of God in heaven. "By his own blood, he entered in once into the holy place, having obtained eternal redemption for us." (Hebrews 9:12) "Christ is not entered into the holy places made with hands, which are figures of the true, but into heaven itself, now to appear in the presence of God for us." (Hebrews 9:24) The tabernacle is a key symbol in the book of Revelation. (Hebrews 9:2-9)

Christ has redeemed us ***"out of every kindred and tongue, and people and nation." 5:9*** God had promised Abraham: "In your seed shall all the nations of the earth be blessed." (Gen. 22:18) This is the theme of the Bible.

The promise was made to Abraham, Isaac, and Jacob. (Gen. 26:4, 28:14) Paul's defense before King Agrippa was the hope of this promise. (Acts 26:6-7) Christ is the "seed" in whom all the nations of the earth will be blessed. (Galatians 3:8, 16, 26-29) The blessing is the forgiveness of sins through his blood. (Acts 2:38-39, Acts 3:25-26) Paul declared that the promise has been fulfilled in Jesus Christ. (Acts 13:32-38)

Christ has **made us unto our God kings and priests; and we shall reign on the earth. 5:10** Christians are now "a royal priesthood." (1 Peter 2:9) As King of kings, Christ is on the throne in heaven. The redeemed are now in the kingdom of Christ and are reigning on the earth. (Col. 1:13-14) They are victorious! (Rev. 1:6)

Then John saw an infinite number of **angels around the throne. 5:11** With a loud voice, they were praising the Lamb for his work of redemption, saying: *"**Worthy is the Lamb that was slain to receive power, and riches, and wisdom, and strength, and honor, and glory, and blessing.**"* **5:12**

Then every created being in heaven and on earth praised God the Father and Christ the Lamb, saying: **"Blessing, and honor, and glory, and power, be to him who sits upon the throne, and to the Lamb, forever and ever." 5:13** When we are feeling defeated and are tempted to think that evil is the victor, let us recall this vision of the open door in heaven with God on his throne.

Then the four living creatures said, "Amen!" And the twenty-four elders fell down and worshiped Him who lives forever and ever. **5:14** NKJV The word "amen" means "so let it be." Let us also worship and serve our God. May we say, "Amen! Let it be so!"

NOTES

Review Questions on Lesson 3

1. The 2nd view is The Seven _____.

2. John saw an open _____ in heaven.

3. How do we know that John was seeing a symbolic view of heaven and not the real place? _____
   _____
   _____

4. What three symbols describe God on the throne?
   _____
   _____
   _____

5. Who are the twenty-four elders representing? _____
   _____

6. The seven lamps of fire symbolize the _____
   _____.

7. The sea of glass before the throne was like the basin of water before the _____.

8. The sea of glass was like crystal, representing _____ and _____.

9. What other symbols are from the tabernacle? _____
   _____
   _____

10. What are the four living creatures representing?
    _____

11. What was in the right hand of God on the throne?
    _____

12. Why did John weep? _____
_____

13. The only one that was able to loose the seven seals was _____.

14. What two animals symbolize Christ? _____ and _____

15. What in Revelation 5:6 symbolizes the resurrection of Christ? _____

16. What do the seven horns of the Lamb symbolize?
_____

17. The prayers of the saints are symbolized by golden bowls full of _____.

18. Praise to the Lord is symbolized by a _____.

19. The twenty-four elders sung a _____ song.

20. What in 5:9 shows the fulfillment of "the promise" made to Abraham, Isaac, and Jacob? _____
_____

The Seven Seals
Revelation 6 – 7

In Revelation 1:18, Jesus said, *"I am he who lives, and was dead, and behold, I am alive forevermore."* We will use this key to interpret the seven seals. In the Book of Revelation, three periods are seen over and over again: **a time of evangelism** like the three-and-a-half years of Christ's ministry, followed by **a short time of severe persecution** as in his death, and then **a time of victory** as in his resurrection.

The Four Horses, Seals 1 – 4
Revelation 6:1-8

Since the common symbol is a horse, the first four seals cover the same period. The fact that it takes four seals suggests that it is the longer time of evangelism. The fifth seal is the brief time of persecution, because slain saints are told that their brethren would be killed for *a little season*. (6:11) The sixth seal brings God's wrath upon those who persecute Christians and so signifies victory for Christ and his church. (6:12-17) The opening of the seventh seal, including the sounding of the seventh trumpet, brings the ultimate victory. (8:1-6; 11:15-18) By using this key to interpret Revelation, we are able to see the unity of the book.

The First Seal – A White Horse
Revelation 6:1-2

When the first seal was opened, John saw *a white horse. And he who sat on him had a bow; and a crown was given to him: and he went forth conquering, and to conquer.* **6:1-2** The white horse is a symbol of victory. The white horse appears again in Revelation 19:11, and its rider is called "Faithful and True" and "The Word of

God". We know that the rider on the white horse is Jesus Christ, because he is "the faithful and true witness" in Revelation 3:14, and he is "the Word" in John 1:1-14.

Some think that the white horse under the first seal is not the same one that is in Revelation 19, because the rider in chapter 6 has a bow, but the rider in chapter 19 has a sword. However, this is a false assumption. In Psalm 45:3-7, the Messiah is described as "the mighty one" who rides "forth victoriously in behalf of truth, humility and righteousness." ^{NIV} He uses both a sword and a bow. His "sword" is mentioned in verse three, and his "arrows" in verse five. Hebrews 1:8-9 quotes verses six and seven of this psalm to describe the supremacy of the Son of God.

Christ has the victor's wreath in 6:2, because he is conquering with the gospel. His many crowns are diadems in 19:12, because he is the King. Different symbols may be used to represent the same person. If Christ can be both the Lion and the Lamb in chapter 5, then Christ as the rider of the white horse can have both a bow in his hand and a sword going out of his mouth. If he can wear "many crowns" on his head, he can wear also the victor's wreath. Two different things are emphasized with figurative language in these two visions about Christ—his victory in evangelism and his sovereign power on the Day of Judgment.

This interpretation agrees with the theme of the book: ***"These shall make war with the Lamb, and the Lamb shall overcome them: for he is Lord of lords, and King of kings: and they that are with him are called, and chosen, and faithful." Revelation 17:14***

During the period of evangelism, Christ is conquering with the gospel that is being preached by his church. This is a spiritual battle. As Paul wrote, "The weapons we fight with are not weapons of the world. On the contrary, they have divine power to demolish strongholds. We demolish arguments and every pretension that sets itself up against the knowledge of God, and we take captive every thought to make it obedient to Christ." (2 Cor. 10:4-5) NIV Hearts are pierced by the gospel. (Acts 2:37) As Christians, we are to "fight the good fight of faith." (1 Timothy 6:12) The white horse symbolizes the victory through evangelism.

Some object to Christ being the rider on the white horse under the first seal, because "the white horse marches the same way as the others."[39] However, Jesus had oppositions and trials during his earthly ministry. Christians also will face difficulties during the long period of evangelism. The other three horses introduce hardships and sufferings that may discipline Christians and lead unbelieving sinners to repentance.

The Second Seal – A Red Horse
Revelation 6:3-4

When the second seal was opened, *a red horse* went out. Its rider was allowed *to take peace from the earth, and that they should kill one another.* To him was given *a great sword.* **6:3-4** The red horse symbolizes war.

Hendriksen has the red horse and its rider representing religious persecutions rather than war, because he insists that the Greek word *machaira* translated "sword" must signify a sacrificial knife.[40] However, this is not the case. The "two-edged sword" that is compared with the word of God in Hebrews 4:12 is the *machaira.* The whole armor of God in Ephesians 6:11-17 includes this sword as the word of God. A soldier having a helmet, a

---

[39] Ray Summers, *Worthy is the Lamb,* p. 140
[40] W. Hendriksen, *More Than Conquerors,* pp. 121-122

breastplate, and a shield used the *machaira* sword. The Roman legionaries used this short, double-edged sword.[41] Jesus said the inhabitants of Jerusalem would fall by the edge of the *machaira* sword when the Roman army destroyed their city, according to Luke 21:20-24. This was an act of divine judgment rather than religious persecution. When Christians are persecuted, they do not kill others. The rider of the red horse has a **great sword** to take peace from the earth, and that they should kill one another. This describes war.

The red horse of war is in the same long period as the white horse of evangelism. While conquering with Christ, the church will endure the sufferings and hardships caused by war. However, the gospel has been received more readily in wartime than in peacetime.

The Third Seal – A Black Horse
Revelation 6:5-6

John saw ***a black horse*** when the third seal was opened, and its rider had ***a pair of balance scales*** in his hand. John heard a voice from among the four living creatures, saying, ***"A quart of wheat for a denarius, and three quarts of barley for a denarius; and do not harm the oil and the wine." 6:5-6*** NKJV The black horse symbolizes economic hardships. One day's wage could buy only one quart of wheat. (Matthew 20:2) If a worker bought the cheaper barley, he could feed his family for a day. Oil and wine were luxuries for the rich. The church at Smyrna was experiencing poverty in the midst of a wealthy city. (2:9) While the church is able to preach the gospel, it may suffer scarcity along with the poor, while the rich have plenty of luxuries. Prosperity may tempt us to forget God, but men turn to God during hard times.

---

[41] Addison-Wesley, *World History Traditions,* 1991 ed., pp. 120-121

The Fourth Seal – A Pale Horse
Revelation 6:7-8

When the fourth seal was opened, *a pale horse* came forth. The name of its rider was *Death, and Hades followed with him. And power was given to them over the fourth part of the earth, to kill with sword, with hunger, and with death, and with the beasts of the earth.* **6:7-8**

The pale horse symbolizes death in its many forms. Hades, the temporary place of the dead, was following the pale horse. During the long period of evangelism, Christians will suffer death like others in various ways—by murder, famine, natural causes or by wild beasts. The sword here is the long sword that was in Old Testament times. Joab used this sword (*rhomphaia*) to commit murder. (1 Kings 2:32 in the Greek Septuagint) Death causes the living to consider their spiritual needs and to be more receptive to God. (Ecclesiastes 7:1-4)

When the Lamb opens the first four seals, the four living creatures take turns introducing the four horses. The better Greek texts have these cherubim addressing the horses, not John, with the simple command, *"Come."* The description of each living creature in Revelation 4:7 fits the horse that he sends out. The first living creature was *like a lion*, and he calls forth the white horse with its rider Jesus Christ, who is "the Lion of the tribe of Judah." (5:5) The second living creature was *like a calf* that is slaughtered, and he calls forth the red horse symbolizing the slaughter in war. "The sword is drawn; for the slaughter it is furbished." (Ezekiel 21:28) The third living creature having *a face as a man* summons the black horse that represents man in his struggles to overcome economic hardships that began when man first sinned. (Genesis 3:17-19) The fourth living creature, who is *like a flying eagle,* sends forth the pale horse indicating the swiftness of death in various forms.

"The Four Horsemen," according to the popular view, personify the four major plagues of mankind,[42] but this is not possible since Christ is the rider on the white horse. The sufferings of war, economic hardships, and death are associated with the other three horsemen, but as we have shown, these trials help those that are lost to see that they need Christ and the gospel of salvation.

Satan causes wars, hardships, diseases, and death, but God limits Satan's destructive powers and uses them for his own purposes.[43] God uses sufferings to warn sinners with the seven trumpets, chapters 8-11, and to punish them with the seven bowls of wrath in chapter 16. In the midst of these hard times, the Christian is given assurance and blessing. "Blessed is he who watches, and keeps his garments." (16:15) He is riding with Christ to victory!

Slain Saints, Seal 5
Revelation 6:9-11

When the fifth seal was opened, John saw *the souls* of martyred Christians *under the altar.* They had been *slain for the word of God* and for confessing their faith in Christ. **6:9** They were like the animal sacrifices whose blood was poured out at the base of the altar before the door of the Old Testament tabernacle. (Leviticus 4:7) The scene has changed. Christians are no longer riding with Christ under the first seal and conquering with the gospel. The church is in **a period of persecution** that compares to the time when Jesus was dead. The voice of the church has been silenced. Christians appear to be hopelessly defeated. When Revelation was written, the church was

---

[42] *Webster's Ninth New Collegiate Dictionary,* 1987, p. 487
[43] Job 1:9-12, Job 2:4-6, Job 33:29-30

Revelation 6-7 | **57**

under the fifth seal. John had been exiled to the island of Patmos "for the word of God, and for the testimony of Jesus Christ." (1:9)

These martyred Christians ask, *"How long, O Lord, holy and true, do you not judge and avenge our blood on them that dwell on the earth?"* **6:10** They are not crying out for personal vengeance, but for proof that they did not die in vain. They need to be reassured of the victory in Jesus.

And white robes, symbolizing purity and victory, *were given to every one of them.* And they were instructed *that they should rest yet for a little season* until the number of their brethren that were to be killed was completed. **6:11** The *rest* here refers to death as in other passages, including Revelation 14:13. After a little while, they are figuratively resurrected, and they reign with Christ in heaven during the period of evangelism that has returned on earth. (20:4-6) Christians should be comforted by the message of the fifth seal whenever they are suffering severely because of unbelievers. They may be tempted to feel that their labors are all in vain. But the time of persecution is only for *a little season,* and then comes the victory! In the book of Revelation, periods of persecution are always for a short time— "three-and-a-half days" (11:7-11), "a short time" (12:12), and "a little season" (20:3, 20:7-9). Christian suffering is like the three days that Jesus was in the tomb, just a little while, and then came the victory in his resurrection!

The Day of God's Wrath, Seal 6
Revelation 6:12-17

When the sixth seal was opened, John saw *a great earthquake; and the sun became black..., and the moon became as blood, and the stars of heaven fell unto the earth ... and the heavens departed as a scroll when it is rolled together, and every mountain and island were moved out of their places.* And the wicked were filled with fear, *for the great day of his wrath is come.* **6:12-17**

Under the sixth seal, God is punishing the persecutors of the church. For Christians, it is a day of victory! They will be able to openly worship and preach the gospel again. (10:11) For the slain saints who have been under the altar during the time of the fifth seal, it is a day of a symbolic resurrection to reign with Christ for a symbolic thousand years in heaven. (20:4-6) The key to the book is in Revelation 1:18. Jesus says, **"I am he who lives, and was dead, and behold, I am alive forevermore."** Just as Christ was raised from the dead, the church that has been figuratively dead will be restored to life under the sixth seal. Christians will be able to evangelize the world again as they did under the first seal. This cycle that occurred ten times during the days of the Roman Empire will happen in various places throughout the Christian Age until Christ's Second Coming.

"The day of the Lord" describes God's removal of rulers and nations from power. This phrase appears twenty-seven times in the Old Testament.[44] In Haggai 2:21-22, the Lord says, "I will shake the heavens and the earth; and I will overthrow the throne of kingdoms, and I will destroy the strength of the kingdoms of the heathen." Joel predicted "the day of the Lord" during his time, saying, "The earth shall quake before them; the heavens shall tremble: the sun and the moon shall be dark, and the stars shall withdraw their shining. ... The sun shall be turned into darkness, and the moon into blood, before the great and the terrible day of the Lord comes." (Joel 2:1, 10, 31) In Joel's time, the day of the Lord was the execution of wicked Athaliah, who had usurped the throne of Judah. For Revelation's first readers, the day of the Lord under

---

[44] Isaiah 13:6-22; Ezekiel 30:3-26; Amos 5:18-20; Zeph. 1:7-18

the sixth seal would be the death of Domitian, who was persecuting them. When Domitian was killed, his loyal followers were afraid.

These days of the Lord in history prefigure the last great day of the Lord at the end of time. The final day of the Lord will come when the seventh seal is opened and the seventh trumpet sounds. (Rev. 8:1; 11:15-19) This day is described in 11:18, *"Your wrath is come, and the time of the dead, and that they should be judged, and that you should give reward unto your servants."* The great day of wrath under the sixth seal is not the final judgment. The seventh seal has not been opened.

At the end of chapter six, the question is asked, *"And who shall be able to stand?"* **6:17** The two visions in chapter seven provide the answer to the question. The first vision gives reassurance to God's people in the day of wrath. The second vision shows the redeemed enjoying the blessings of heaven. This interval between the opening of the sixth and seventh seals is for the purpose of encouraging God's people to remain faithful.

The Vision of the 144,000
Revelation 7:1-8

After these things, I saw four angels standing on the four corners of the earth, holding the four winds of the earth, that the wind should not blow on the earth, nor on the sea, nor on any tree. **7:1** Destructive winds may come from all four directions—north, east, south, and west. But God's angels are in control of them. There are winds of disasters on land and sea. There are winds of diseases and death. If it were not for God's angels restraining these winds, we would have a constant flood of calamities. As our adversary, the devil desires to harm us. (1 Peter 5:8) But God controls the destructive powers of Satan and uses them for his own purposes when he chooses. (Ezekiel 5:11-17) When the seven trumpets sound in chapters 8-11 and when the seven bowls of wrath are poured out upon the earth in chapter 16, these destructive winds are unleashed.

Then John saw *another angel ascending from the east, having the seal of the living God.* **7:2** As the sun rises in the east promising a new day, the angel ascends from the east promising a new life in heaven. The seal is used to show ownership, authority and protection.

This angel cried with a loud voice to the four angels, *"Hurt not the earth, neither the sea, nor the trees, till we have sealed the servants of our God in their foreheads."* **7:2-3** The sealing of God's servants is showing that they belong to God. We are given these words of assurance in 2 Timothy 2:19, "Nevertheless the foundation of God stands sure, having this seal. The Lord knows those that are his." In the tabernacle, the high priest wore on his forehead the words **"Holiness to the Lord"** engraved upon a golden plate. (Exodus 28:36-38) As the high priest went about his duties, he was reminded that he belonged to God. God's people are not wearing a literal engraving or sign, but they have sanctified the Lord God in their hearts, according to 1 Peter 3:15. Those that have God's seal show by their lives that they belong to him. In Revelation 13, those that have the mark of the beast show by their actions that they belong to Satan. As Jesus said, "He that is not with me is against me." (Matthew 12:30)

When the destructive winds are allowed to blow, we should not consider our suffering to be punishment for sin if we are faithfully serving the Lord. God has not forsaken us. Don't lose heart! "For our light affliction, which is but for a moment, works for us a far more exceeding and eternal weight of glory; while we look not at the things which are seen, but at the things which are not seen: for the things which are seen are temporal; but the things which are not seen are eternal." (2 Corinthians 4:17-18) When this earth is destroyed, we shall enjoy "new heavens and a new earth, wherein dwells righteousness." (2 Peter 3:10-13)

The number of those that were sealed was *a hundred and forty-four thousand of all the tribes of the children of Israel.* **7:4-8** Twelve thousand were sealed from each of the twelve tribes of Israel. Both the 12,000 and the 144,000 have symbolic meaning.

Twelve is the symbolic number for God's people. The heavenly city, the New Jerusalem in Revelation 21, has twelve gates representing the twelve tribes of Israel of the old covenant and twelve foundations representing the twelve apostles of the new covenant. (21:2, 10-14)

The holy city of God is a cube in shape— "the length, and the breadth, and the height of it are equal." (21:16) The Most Holy Place represented the presence of God in the Tabernacle. It also was a cube in shape—ten cubits by ten cubits by ten cubits. One thousand, a perfect number, is the product of ten times ten times ten. Therefore, **one thousand is the symbolic number for heaven**, God's perfect dwelling place. Knowing this will help us to understand the book of Revelation.

Twelve thousand symbolizes God's people, who are going to heaven. There were twelve thousand from each of the twelve tribes of Israel making a total of 144,000. If the number is symbolic, so Israel also is symbolic. Will only those of physical Israel be saved? Certainly not! "For they are not all Israel, which are of Israel." (Romans 9:6) The tribe of Dan is not included in the 144,000, because Dan was the first tribe to go into idolatry. (Judges 18:30) In its place the priestly tribe of Levi, which did not receive a land inheritance, is among the twelve tribes of the 144,000. The unfaithful are not sealed; they are not going to heaven!

The word *Israel* means power with God. Who has power with God today? Christians are God's "holy nation, His own special people." (1 Peter 2:9) ^{NKJV} They are "the Israel of God" in Galatians 6:15-16.

Who are the 144,000? They are the "redeemed from the earth" in Revelation 14:3. Jesus Christ the Lamb has redeemed us to God by his blood "from every tribe and language and people and nation." (5:9) ^{NIV} **The 144,000 are the redeemed of the earth from every tribe and nation—not just physical Israel.** So, all of God's people (12) from all the tribes of the earth (12) that are going to heaven (1,000) make up the symbolic 144,000.

The Vision of the Great Multitude
Revelation 7:9-17

After this I beheld, and lo, a great multitude, which no one could number, of all nations, and kindreds, and peoples and tongues, stood before the throne. **7:9** This vision plainly reveals that those going to heaven will not be limited to a literal 144,000. The saved in heaven are a multitude that cannot be numbered. Spiritual Israel is the redeemed from all nations—not just physical Israel.

These faithful saints are clothed with *white robes* that symbolize purity and victory. The *palm* branches in their hands are symbols of joy. (Lev. 23:40) They are saying, **"Salvation to our God who sits upon the throne, and to the Lamb." 7:9-10** All of the trials of earthly life are over. Now is the time to enjoy salvation in heaven with God. All the angels around the throne and the elders and the four living creatures fall on their faces before the throne and worship God. They praise God with thanksgiving for saving the great multitude. **7:11-12**

Then one of the elders asked John, *"Who are these arrayed in white robes, and where did they come from?"* He wanted John to understand the meaning of these symbols. He told him that those in the white robes are *"the ones who come out of the great tribulation."* **7:13-14** NKJV The tribulation is great because it includes all the trials and persecutions God's people have suffered on the earth. The elder added, *"They have washed their robes and made them white in the blood of the Lamb."* **7:14** The saved have been redeemed by the blood of Christ!

"Therefore they are before the throne of God, and serve him day and night in his temple: and he that sits on the throne shall dwell among them." **7:15** Heaven is a place of service to God by his servants continually. God will be with his people, or literally "will spread his tent over them" as in the NIV. Our being in the presence of God will be the greatest blessing of heaven.

"They shall hunger no more, neither thirst anymore; neither shall the sun light on them, nor any heat; for the Lamb who is in the midst of the throne shall feed them, and shall lead them unto living fountains of waters: and God shall wipe away all tears from their eyes." **7:16-17** All needs are fulfilled; all pain and sorrows are removed. These words are similar to those in Revelation 21:3-6. This is proof that Revelation gives us parallel views. With the vision of the great multitude before the throne of God in heaven, we have come to the end of the second view of the victorious church.

NOTES

Review Questions on Lesson 4

1. The rider of the white horse is _____.

2. The red horse and its rider symbolize _____.

3. The black horse is for _____ _____.

4. The pale horse and its rider symbolize _____.

5. The four _____ _____ send out the horses.

6. Seals 1-4 are in the period of _____ that is like the 3 ½ year _____ of Christ.

7. What did John see when the fifth seal was opened?
   _____

8. Under the 5th Seal, the church is in the short period of _____ that's like when Jesus was _____.

9. Under the 6th Seal, God punishes the _____ of the church; it is a day of _____ for Christians.

10. What does "the day of the Lord" describe?
    _____
    _____

11. Why is the 6th Seal not describing the last great day of the Lord at the end of time? _____
    _____

12. What question in 6:17 is answered in chapter seven?
    _____

13. Four angels were holding back the four destructive winds so they would not blow on the _____.

66 | The Seven Seals

14. Who were to be sealed in their foreheads? 7:3
    _____

15. Having "the seal of God" means you _____ to God.

16. The symbolic number for God's people is _____;
    the symbolic number for heaven is _____.

17. What does *twelve thousand* symbolize?
    _____

18. What is symbolized by the omission of the tribe of Dan?
    _____

19. What does *Israel* mean? _____

20. Who are the symbolic 144,000? _____
    _____

21. How do we know from 7:9 that the redeemed in heaven is not a literal 144,000 of physical Israel?
    _____
    _____

22. How had the robes of the saved been made white?
    _____

23. How does Revelation 7:9-17 prove that the book contains parallel views? _____
    _____

View 3

The Seven Trumpets

Revelation 8 – 11

NOTES

The Seven Trumpets
Revelation 8 – 9

In the Bible, the purpose of sounding a trumpet is either to warn or to announce. Amos 3:6 asks, "Shall a trumpet be blown in the city, and the people not be afraid?" The trumpet of God will announce the Second Coming of Christ. (1 Thess. 4:16) The natural calamities that follow the sounding of the trumpets are warnings to unbelievers that the Lord's judgment is coming. In the time of Amos, God warned sinners with hunger, drought, blight and mildew, locusts, disease, fire, and war. Yet they did not return to him. So he said, "Prepare to meet your God, O Israel." (Amos 4:6-12) Because they would not repent, the day of the Lord came. They were sent into captivity beyond Damascus. (Amos 5:27) In the third parallel view, the seventh seal reveals the seven trumpets.

And when he had opened the seventh seal, there was silence in heaven about the space of half an hour. **8:1** The purpose of silence was to emphasize the judgments and warnings that were about to follow. "The LORD is in his holy temple: let all the earth keep silence before him." (Habakkuk 2:20) "Be silent in the presence of the Lord for the day of the Lord is at hand." (Zephaniah 1:7) NKJV

Then John saw ***the seven angels which stood before God; and to them were given seven trumpets. And another angel came and stood at the altar, having a golden censer; and there was given to him much incense, that he should offer it with the prayers of all saints upon the golden altar which was before the throne.*** **8:2-3** The golden altar of incense is another symbol from the Old Testament tabernacle and should not be interpreted literally. In heaven, there will not be a golden altar of incense. The Old Testament tabernacle "was symbolic for the present time." (Heb. 9:9) ᴺᴷᴶⱽ "But Christ came as High Priest of the good things to come, with a greater and more perfect tabernacle not made with hands, that is, not of this creation." (Heb. 9:11) ᴺᴷᴶⱽ

As the saints prayed *the smoke of the incense ascended up before* **God. 8:4** The smoke represents the intercessions of Christ for Christians when they pray. (1 John 2:1, Heb. 7:25, John 14:13) Incense was offered on the golden altar at the hour of prayer. (Luke 1:10)

Then the angel took the censer and filled it with fire from the altar and threw it on the earth; and there were peals of thunder, rumblings, flashes of lightning and an earthquake. **8:5** ᴱˢⱽ The prayers of Christians are heard and answered through God's control and use of natural events upon the earth. Prayers are powerful and effective in the world. Elijah "prayed earnestly that it might not rain: and it rained not on the earth for the space of three years and six months." (James 5:17) The seven trumpets are sounded in answer to prayers.

And the seven angels which had the seven trumpets prepared themselves to sound. **8:6** Amos 3:6 asks, "If a trumpet is blown, will not the people be afraid? If there is a calamity, will not the Lᴏʀᴅ have done it?" ᴺᴷᴶⱽ God uses natural events to warn sinners to repent. Nero's bloody persecution of Christians lasted from AD 64 to 68. During this period and up to the eruption of Vesuvius in AD 79, a series of earthquakes alarmed the people in that area.[45] These earthquakes and the violent destruction of Pompeii and Herculaneum with lava and volcanic ash should have been a warning to the Romans. The sounding of each trumpet signals the four angels that are in Revelation 7:1 to release a destructive wind to harm the earth or the sea. The symbols are related.

---

[45] *The World Book Encyclopedia*, 1974 edition, Volume 20, p. 270

The First Four Trumpets

The first angel sounded, and there followed hail and fire mingled with blood, and they were cast upon the earth: and the third part of trees was burnt up, and all green grass was burnt up. **8:7** Death would come from these calamities because they were "mingled with blood." The seventh plague upon the Egyptians was hail and fire. (Exodus 9:24) This is not the final Day of Judgment because only some of the trees were burned up. The natural **disasters on land**, such as hail and fire, should warn sinners to repent!

And the second angel sounded, and as it were a great mountain burning with fire was cast into the sea: and a third part of the sea became blood; and the third part of the creatures which were in the sea, and had life, died; and the third of the ships were destroyed. **8:8-9** A storm at sea was caused by Jonah's disobedience. God sent the storm to warn Jonah and the people of Nineveh. (Jonah 1:4-10, Matt. 12:41) The natural **disasters at sea** should be a warning to sinners to repent!

And the third angel sounded, and there fell a great star from heaven, burning as it were a lamp, and it fell upon the third part of the rivers and upon the fountains of waters; and the name of the star is called Wormwood: and the third part of the waters became wormwood; and many men died of the waters, because they were made bitter. **8:10-11** The great fiery star falling from heaven is a way of saying that the calamity is a messenger from God. Wormwood is associated with gall or bitterness and affliction in Lamentations 3:19. The Lord would feed his disobedient people with wormwood, and give them water of gall (or poisonous water) to drink in Jeremiah 9:15. Rivers and springs become polluted causing sickness and death. The **pollution of fresh waters** should warn sinners to repent!

***And the fourth angel sounded, and a third of the sun was smitten, and a third of the moon, and a third of the stars; so as the third of them was darkened.* 8:12** Solar and lunar eclipses, storms, and volcanic eruptions can darken the sky. On Paul's sea voyage to Rome, "when neither the sun nor stars in many days appeared" because of the great storm at sea, those who were with Paul gave up all hope of being saved. (Acts 27:20) The **disturbances in the sky** should warn sinners of their need to repent!

The Remaining Trumpets

***Then John saw an eagle flying through the midst of heaven, and he heard the eagle saying with a loud voice, "Woe! Woe! Woe to the inhabitants of the earth, because of the trumpet blasts about to be sounded by the other three angels!"* 8:13** ᴺᴵⱽ An *eagle* instead of *angel* makes this announcement, according to the better text. Perhaps the fourth living creature that "was like a flying eagle" is the angel who is speaking. (4:7) The "woes" are the last three trumpets. The worst is yet to come.

***And the fifth angel blew his trumpet, and I saw a star fallen from heaven to the earth, and he was given the key to the shaft of the bottomless pit.* 9:1** ᴱˢⱽ A *star* is the symbol for an angel. (1:20) John saw a *fallen* angel. The angel's present condition is the result of past action because the Greek word for *fallen* is a participle in the perfect tense. He had rebelled against God. (Jude 6) This fallen angel is Satan. (Luke 10:18, Rev. 12:9)

The *bottomless pit* is the intermediate prison for fallen spirits. In 2 Peter 2:4, the Greek word translated *"hell"* is *Tartarus,* the place where the wicked angels have been cast down and are now in "chains of darkness, to be reserved for judgment." The *abyss* is another name for the bottomless pit, the abode of the devil and his angels along with the demons. (Luke 8:30-31) It is mentioned again in Revelation 11:7, 17:8 and 20:1-3. In Revelation 20:7, it is called the *prison* of Satan. It is not the lake of fire—the final destination of fallen spirits. (Rev. 14:9-11, Rev. 20:10-15)

Satan *"was given"* the key. God allows Satan to unlock the prison of the pit and unleash evil influences. This fallen angel to whom *"was given"* the key should not be confused with the angel of God *"having"* the key in Revelation 20:1. God permits Satan to carry out some of his wicked desires in the lives of men in order to punish them for their sins and to warn them of their ultimate doom if they do not repent. God has control over the key to the bottomless pit, because he has the keys to Hades and Death. (Rev. 1:18)

***And he opened the bottomless pit; and there arose a smoke out of the pit, as the smoke of a great furnace; and the sun and the air were darkened by reason of the smoke of the pit.* 9:2** The smoke represents temptations, Satan's falsehoods that entice men to sin. (Genesis 3:4) Like the smoke that hides the sun, these deceptions keep us from seeing what is true, pure, and good. Sin is deceitful, according to Hebrews 3:13. The lies of Satan pollute the environment and cause those who do not love the truth to perish. (2 Thess. 2:10-12)

***And there came out of the smoke locusts upon the earth.* 9:3** The locusts are symbolic of fully developed sins that come out of temptations. ***And unto them was given power, as the scorpions of the earth have power. And it was commanded them that they should not hurt the grass of the earth, neither any green thing, neither any tree; but only those men which have not the seal of God in their foreheads.* 9:3-4** These are not literal, physical locusts that devour vegetation; they are the sins that destroy the lives of men!

And to them it was given that they should not kill them, but that they should be tormented five months. **9:5** Even when Satan is allowed some freedom, his activities are restricted. (Job 1:12, Job 2:6) Five months is the life span of locusts. Sinners will be tormented by their sins as long as they continue in them.

Their torment was as the torment of a scorpion when he strikes a man. And in those days men shall seek death, and shall not find it; and shall desire to die, and death shall flee from them. **9:5-6** The scorpion sting brings great pain, but it does not kill. The torment of sin is both physical and mental. There is no relief from this intense pain. The suffering is so intense that men desire death, but they are denied it.

The shape of the locusts was like horses prepared for battle. On their heads were crowns of something like gold, and their faces were the faces of men. **9:7** NKJV Sin seems so impressive and powerful. The locusts have victors' crowns (*stephanoi*). Satan says, "If you want to win, you must sin." But these crowns are made of ***something like gold.*** They're not real, but artificial and imitative. The victory is in Christ and his righteousness! We are tempted through other human beings, because the faces of the locusts were the faces of men.

And they had hair as the hair of women, and their teeth were as the teeth of lions. **9:8** The temptations of sin may be attractive and beautiful, but they are deadly like a lion's teeth.

And they had breastplates, as it were breastplates of iron; and the sound of their wings was as the sound of chariots of many horses running to battle. **9:9** Satan's first recorded lie was "You will not surely die" if you disobey God. He wants us to feel invincible. (Gen. 3:4)

And they had tails like unto scorpions, and there were stings in their tails. **9:10** Sin at first appears very desirable, but its end is pain and misery. "There is a way which seems right unto a man, but the end thereof is the way of death." (Prov. 14:12) "Do not look on the wine when it is red, when it sparkles in the cup, when it swirls around smoothly; at the last it bites like a serpent and stings like a viper." (Proverbs 23:31-32) ᴺᴷᴶⱽ

And they had a king over them, which is the angel of the bottomless pit, whose name in the Hebrew tongue is Abaddon, but in the Greek tongue has his name Apollyon. **9:11** The fallen star is now plainly identified as "the angel of the bottomless pit." He is Satan because his Hebrew name means "Destruction" and his Greek name means "Destroyer". Our "adversary the devil" is "seeking whom he may devour." (1 Peter 5:8) **The fifth trumpet** warns sinners with the **sufferings of sin!**

One woe is past; and behold, there come two woes more hereafter. **9:12** The last three trumpets are called three "woes" in Revelation 8:13, because of their intense sufferings.

And the sixth angel sounded, and I heard a voice from the four horns of the golden altar which is before God, saying to the sixth angel which had the trumpet, "Loose the four angels which are bound in the great river Euphrates." **9:13-14** The voice from the altar of incense is in answer to the prayers of the saints. (Rev. 8:3-5) Their cause is vindicated. The four angels that are bound should not be confused with the four angels of God who are holding back the four winds in Revelation 7:1. These are evil angels at the Euphrates River, who plunge men into war when they are released. **9:15-19** As the Romans attempted to stabilize their eastern boundary, the Parthians defeated them in 53 BC and in AD 62. The Euphrates River separated the Roman Empire from this dreadful enemy.⁴⁶ The Euphrates symbolizes all national boundaries that are crossed by invading armies.

And the four angels were loosed, which were prepared for an hour, and a day, and a month, and a year, for to slay the third part of men. **9:15** God is in control of wars. God plans for the exact time, down to the hour, when Satan's destructive angels are released and wars begin. Those killed were a third of men. This is a large number, but this is not total destruction.

And the number of the army of the horsemen was two hundred million. **9:16** ᴺᴬˢᴮ A great army is indicated by this number. God used invading armies during the time of the Judges to cause the nation of Israel to repent.

I saw in the vision the horses and those that sat on them: the riders had breastplates the color of fire and of hyacinth and of brimstone; and the heads of the horses are like the heads of lions; and out of their mouths proceed fire and smoke and brimstone A third of mankind was killed by these three plagues, by the fire, and the smoke, and the brimstone, which proceeded out of their mouths. **9:17-18** ᴺᴬˢᴮ A dreadful army is described symbolically. The fire, the hyacinth (purple) smoke, and the brimstone represent the various weapons of war. To the early readers this army would be the Parthians, Goths, Visigoths, Huns, and Vandals, who invaded Roman territory from time to time.⁴⁷ *For their power is in their mouth, and in their tails.* **9:19** This describes military tactics.

The sixth trumpet warns sinners with **the sufferings of wars!**

---

[46] J. W. Roberts, *The Revelation to John*, p. 82
[47] Stafford North, *Unlocking Revelation*, p. 60

And the rest of the men which were not killed by these plagues repented not of the works of their hands, that they should not worship devils and idols of gold, and silver, and brass, and stone, and of wood, which neither can see, nor hear, nor walk. **9:20-21** As it was in the days of Amos, the majority of those that survive disasters and wars will not repent of their sins, when God uses trumpets to warn them. (Amos 4:10)

Review Questions on Lesson 5

1. The seventh _____ reveals the seven trumpets.

2. The purpose of sounding a trumpet is to _____ and to _____.

3. The prophet _____ said that natural disasters and wars are used by God to warn sinners to repent.

4. The smoke of incense represents the _____ of Christ when we pray.

5. The first trumpet is natural disasters on _____.

6. The second trumpet is natural disasters at _____.

7. The third trumpet is the _____ of rivers and springs of water.

8. The fourth trumpet is disturbances in the _____.

9. The smoke coming from the bottomless pit symbolizes _____.

10. Locusts that come out of the smoke symbolize _____.

11. The fifth trumpet warns with the sufferings of _____.

12. The names of the king of the bottomless pit were: Abaddon meaning _____ and Apollyon meaning _____.

13. Who is the king of the bottomless pit? _____

14. The sixth trumpet warns with the sufferings of _____.

The Little Book
Revelation 10-11

John saw *another mighty angel* coming down from heaven. He was *clothed with a cloud.* And on his head was *a rainbow. His face was as the sun, and his feet as pillars of fire.* **10:1** John had already seen a strong angel in Revelation 5:2. The cloud covering the second mighty angel symbolizes God's judgment. (Rev. 1:7; Zeph. 1:15) The rainbow represents God's mercy. (Gen. 9:11-16) God's righteousness is indicated by the sun. (Mal. 4:2) God's ability to destroy all enemies is seen in the feet like pillars of fire. These symbols describe the angel because they also describe God the Father and Jesus Christ. (Rev. 4:3; Rev. 1:15-16) Those in the presence of God reflect his glory, as did Moses in Exodus 34:29-30. As a messenger of God, the angel possesses judgment, mercy, righteousness, and power to execute God's will.

And he had in his hand a little book open. **10:2** Like the scroll with seven seals, it reveals things to be. It is *little* because it reveals only one theme. It is *open* because its revelation was opened when the scroll with seven seals was opened.

And he set his right foot upon the sea, and his left foot upon the earth. **10:2** The mighty angel is in control of both land and sea. He symbolizes the Providence of God. (Hebrews 1:13-14) God's view of the earth and its events is not man's view. (Isaiah 55:8-9)

The angel *cried with a loud voice, as when a lion roars: and when he had cried, seven thunders uttered their voices.* **10:3** The roar of a lion symbolizes God's warning to the disobedient. (Amos 1:2, 3:4; Joel 3:16) John was about to write what the seven thunders had said, but he heard a voice from heaven saying to him, *"Seal up those things which the seven thunders uttered, and write them not."* **10:4** Some things remain unknown for our own good. "The secret things belong unto the LORD our God, but those things which are revealed belong unto us and to our children forever." (Deuteronomy 29:29)

With his right hand raised toward heaven, the angel swore that the mystery of God spoken by the prophets would be accomplished when the seventh angel sounded his trumpet. **10:5-7** After six trumpets have sounded their warnings, God will delay no longer the final punishment of the wicked. The seventh trumpet announces the Day of Judgment at the end of time. (Rev. 11:15-18) All the prophecies of God's servants the prophets will be fulfilled when the seventh trumpet sounds, but the book of Revelation does not end with chapter eleven. This proves that the book reveals parallel views of the church.

John heard again the voice from heaven speaking to him, saying, *"Go and take the little book which is open in the hand of the angel which stands upon the sea and upon the earth."* So John went to the angel and said to him, *"Give me the little book."* And he said to John, *"Take it, and eat it up; and it shall make your belly bitter, but it will be in your mouth sweet as honey."* Then John took the little book out of the angel's hand and ate it, and it was as sweet as honey in his mouth. But as soon as he had eaten it, his stomach was bitter. **10:8-10** God's word is sweet! "How sweet are your words unto my taste, yea sweeter than honey to my mouth!" (Psalm 119:103) But God reveals that along with the blessings of his word, there are sufferings and hardships to be endured. "For unto you it is given in the behalf of Christ, not only to believe on him, but also to suffer for his sake." (Philippians 1:29) As children of God, we are "heirs of God and joint heirs with Christ, if so be that we suffer with him, that we may be also glorified together."

(Romans 8:17) The prophet Ezekiel also was commanded to eat a scroll in Ezekiel 2:8-9. At first, God's word was "as honey for sweetness" in his mouth, but within the scroll were "lamentations, and mourning, and woe." (Ezekiel 3:3, 2:10)

The *"little book"* contains a bittersweet message to the church that will be introduced in the next chapter and will become the theme of the last half of the book of Revelation.

The angel said to John, **"You must prophesy again before many peoples, and nations, and tongues, and kings." 10:11** The Greek word translated *before* is *epi*, which also may be translated *to*. Hugo McCord gives a good translation of this verse: "You must prophesy again *to* peoples and nations and languages and many kings."[48] At the time of the writing of Revelation, John was not able to preach. He was "in the tribulation" as an exile on Patmos. (1:9) The message of the "little book" was at first sweet with the good news that he would be able to preach again. But in time, there would be bitterness with the return of persecution against the church by the Roman Emperor Trajan. This would be a repeating cycle of *sweet* (evangelism) and *bitter* (persecution).

John was given a reed for a measuring rod. And the angel stood saying, **"Rise, and measure the temple of God, and the altar, and them that worship therein." 11:1** John could not measure the physical temple in Jerusalem, because in AD 70, the Romans had destroyed it. In a vision, John saw the temple of God. The Greek word translated *temple* is *naos*, which is used only of the sanctuary itself—the Holy Place and the Most Holy Place. It is to be distinguished from the whole temple.[49]

---

[48] Hugo McCord, *McCord's New Testament Translation*, p. 469
[49] Joseph H. Thayer, *Greek-English Lexicon*, (1962), **"naos"**, p. 422

The Holy Place and the Most Holy Place symbolize the church and heaven. Only the priests entered the Holy Place, and only Christians are serving as a holy priesthood in the church. (1 Peter 2:5-9) The church is God's spiritual temple.[50] John uses a measuring rod, the word of God, to give assurance to the Lord's church of their hope in heaven. Measuring symbolizes protection.[51] The altar symbolizes the privilege and power of prayer. Those who are true worshipers in the Lord's church will be protected against all opposition.

***But the court which is without the temple leave out, and measure it not, for it is given unto the Gentiles.* 11:2** The congregation of Israel met in this court. Those Jews who would not come into the church would be left outside of God's protection and become part of the unbelieving Gentiles. In a dramatic way God had already demonstrated the removal of his protection from physical Israel when the Romans destroyed both the temple and Jerusalem in AD 70. Only the church and heaven remain as the true spiritual sanctuary of God.[52]

***And the holy city shall they tread underfoot forty-two months. And I will give power to my two witnesses, and they shall prophesy a thousand two hundred and sixty days, clothed in sackcloth.* 11:2-3** The symbolism of three-and-a-half years is introduced in these verses. The 42 months equal three-and-a-half years. The Jewish calendar had 30 days in a month. The product of multiplying 42 months by 30 days is 1,260 days. Therefore, the 42 months and the 1,260 days are describing the same period of three-and-a-half years. The significance of this number of years begins in the Old Testament.

---

[50] 1 Corinthians 3:16; 2 Corinthians 6:16; Ephesians 2:20
[51] Rubel Shelly, *The Lamb and his Enemies,* p. 64
[52] Hebrews 8:1-2; Hebrews 9:11

King Ahab and his wicked wife Jezebel led the nation of Israel into the idolatrous worship of Baal, during the time of the prophet Elijah. (1 Kings 16:30-33) "Baal was the farm god who gave increase to family and field, flocks and herds."[53] To show that only the true God of heaven possesses the power to bless, Elijah "prayed earnestly that it might not rain: and it rained not on the earth by the space of **three years and six months**." (James 5:17) The fields dried up and the cattle died. Although Ahab wanted to find and kill Elijah, God protected him. God's power was displayed at Mt. Carmel with fire from heaven that consumed the sacrifice and the stones of the altar. This great miracle caused the people to believe in the Lord, and they executed the prophets of Baal. (1 Kings 17:1-18:45) To further show the power of God, Elijah "prayed again, and the heaven gave rain, and the earth brought forth her fruit." (James 5:17) This period of three-and-a-half years demonstrated the power of God.

Satan tries to imitate God. In the second century BC, he had his own three-and-a-half years of power. In fulfillment of the prophecies in Daniel 8-12, the Seleucid king Antiochus IV called himself **Epiphanes Theos** meaning "Illustrious God." For three-and-a-half years, from June, 168 BC through December, 165 BC, he took away the temple sacrifices in Jerusalem and made God's temple a shrine to Jupiter.[54] He tried to force the Jews to become pagans and killed over 100,000 that resisted. Women and children were sold into slavery.[55] "Gog and Magog" in Revelation 20:8 is another reference to this wicked king, Antiochus IV, and his persecution of God's people. The Jewish festival of **Hanukkah** commemorates the end of this persecution and the dedication of

---
[53] *The New Unger's Bible Dictionary,* "Baal"
[54] Paul T. Butler, *Daniel,* pp. 455 – 460, and
   Albert Barnes, *Barnes Notes,* Daniel 12:7-11, Biblesoft
[55] *International Standard Bible Encyclopaedia,* "Between the Testaments"

the temple. It is called "The Feast of Dedication" in John 10:22, which is the meaning of the word *Hanukkah*.

God reclaimed this period with the greatest display of his power during the earthly ministry of Jesus, which lasted three-and-a-half years.[56] Jesus walked on the water, calmed the storm, and multiplied loaves and fish. He healed the sick, cast out demons, gave sight to the blind, restored an ear and a withered hand, and even raised the dead. Enemies slandered him and tried to kill him. But Jesus was able to teach and preach, because God was protecting him during these three-and-a-half years of his ministry.

At first, it may seem that the forty-two months is a time of persecution of Christians because "the holy city" will be trodden underfoot. However, we must remember the vision that John was seeing. He saw the temple and the city of Jerusalem. He was instructed to measure the Holy Place (representing the church) and the Most Holy Place (heaven), which is a figurative way of saying that they will be protected. But he was not to measure the court of the temple and Jerusalem because they would not be protected. They would be given over to the Gentiles. The once holy city is representing the Jews who not only crucified our Lord (11:8) but also were the first to persecute Christians. (Acts 4) At this time, the city of Jerusalem was in a state of ruin, having been destroyed by the Romans in AD 70. This was God's judgment against the Jews who did not believe in Jesus Christ and persecuted his church.

God said, *"I will give power unto my two witnesses, and they shall prophesy."* 11:3 The two witnesses represent the evangelism of the church. Jesus sent his

---

[56] J. W. McGarvey, *The Fourfold Gospel*, p. 194. Also see...
Lucian Farrar, Jr., *The Book of Daniel*, "The Most High Rules", p. 91

disciples, two by two, into every city and place to preach. (Luke 10:1-2) Being **clothed in sackcloth** represents their message of repentance. (Luke 10:13, Acts 2:38, Acts 17:30) This is a period of power—not of persecution. This is the time for work—not for reward and glory. During this time the church has power to preach the gospel. Three-and-a-half years represent evangelism.

These are the two olive trees and the two lampstands that stand before the Lord of the earth. **11:4** ᴱˢⱽ This symbolism is from the prophet Zechariah, whom God sent to encourage his people to rebuild the temple in Jerusalem after the Babylonian exile. The two olive trees are "the two anointed ones that stand by the Lord of the whole earth." (Zech. 4:11-14) The two anointed ones in Zechariah's time were Zerubbabel the governor and Joshua the High Priest. Zerubbabel laid the foundation of the temple and his hands finished it. (Zechariah 4:9) Joshua served in the temple, and the Lord removed their iniquity. (Zechariah 3:4-9) As God rebuilt the temple after the Babylonian exile, he will restore his church after being silenced by persecution. The church will be able to preach the gospel again and bring light to the world. God's power will accomplish this work. (Zech. 4:6-10)

And if any man will hurt them, fire proceeds out of their mouth, and devours their enemies. **11:5** As Jesus faced opposition, so will his church. (Matthew 10:25) The unbelieving Jews wanted to kill Jesus, but God protected him in his ministry.[57] During the long period of evangelism, enemies will try to destroy the church, but God will protect his people from harm. The church will be able to preach and defeat its enemies by the "fire" of God's truth. (Jeremiah 5:14) "Go ye into all the world, and preach the gospel to every creature. He that believes

---

[57] John 5:16, John 8:59, John 10:31-39, John 7:30, John 8:20

and is baptized shall be saved; but he that believes not shall be damned." (Mark 16:15-16)

***These have power to shut heaven, that it rain not in the days of their prophecy.* 11:6** This is a direct reference to Elijah when he prayed that it would not rain, and it did not rain for three years and six months. (James 5:17) We began our interpretation of the three-and-a-half years with this event in the prophetic work of Elijah. (See pages 82-83.) God answers the prayers of the faithful. This period symbolizes God's power.

The two witnesses ***have power over waters to turn them to blood, and to smite the earth with all plagues, as often as they will.* 11:6** When Moses delivered the nation of Israel from their bondage in Egypt, God showed his power by bringing ten plagues upon the Egyptians, including turning water into blood. The plagues that followed the sounding of the seven trumpets were in answer to the prayers of the saints. The church is aided in its evangelism by the power of God as were Moses and Elijah, two witnesses from the Old Testament.

***And when they shall have finished their testimony, the beast that ascends out of the bottomless pit shall make war against them, and shall overcome them, and kill them.* 11:7** The beast represents governments and rulers that Satan has deceived to persecute God's people. The bottomless pit is the abode of the devil and his angels. (9:1) Satan has his own resurrection. The beast rising up from the pit is the second resurrection of Revelation 20:7-9. The period of evangelism is over. When the beast makes *war* against the church, it is a time of severe persecution. The church is not able to worship and evangelize publicly. The evangelistic voice of the church has been silenced; it is dead.

And their dead bodies shall lie in the street of the great city, which spiritually is called Sodom and Egypt, where also our Lord was crucified. **11:8** Jesus was crucified in Jerusalem. This once "holy" and "great city" is now spiritually called Sodom because of its sins and Egypt because of its bondage. (Galatians 4:25) This plainly shows that earthly Jerusalem holds no special favor with God. Their dead bodies are in Jerusalem, because wherever Christians are persecuted they are sharing in the sufferings of Christ, who was crucified in that city. (1 Peter 4:12-13) The church was "in the tribulation" when the book of Revelation was being written. (1:9)

Nations shall see their dead bodies three days and a half, and shall not suffer their dead bodies to be put into graves. And they that dwell upon the earth shall rejoice over them and make merry, and shall send gifts one to another, because these two prophets tormented them that dwelt on the earth. **11:9-10** The church torments those of the world by its condemnation of sin and by its message of repentance. The unbelievers show disrespect for the church and rejoice over its being silenced.

After three days and a half the spirit of life from God entered into them, and they stood upon their feet, and great fear fell upon them which saw them. **11:11** This is not a literal, physical resurrection, but a symbolic one. The church is no longer persecuted and silenced. The church that seemed to be dead is alive again and able to teach and preach. John had been banished to the isle of Patmos when he wrote Revelation 1:9, but he was promised, "You must prophesy again." (10:11) The end of the persecution of Christians is "the first resurrection" of Revelation 20:4-6. The revival of the church causes fear in the hearts of the unbelievers because its testimony has been confirmed. The church is victorious!

***And they heard a great voice from heaven saying to them, "Come up." And they ascended up to heaven in a cloud, and their enemies beheld them.* 11:12** Heaven is the ultimate destination for the two witnesses, who represent the church. After faithfully completing their work of evangelism and suffering for the gospel, they will ascend into heaven in a cloud like their Lord. "It is enough for a disciple to be like his teacher, and the servant like his master." (Matthew 10:25) ^{ESV} With the return of evangelism on earth, the dead Christian martyrs live and reign with Christ for a symbolic 1,000 years in heaven. (20:4-6)

Again, the key to Revelation may be seen. Jesus says, ***"I am he who lives, and was dead, and behold, I am alive forevermore."*** (1:18) During the three-and-a-half years of his earthly ministry, Jesus was alive. Although he had opposition and was blasphemed and threatened, he was able to preach. The two witnesses, representing the evangelistic work of the church, are able to preach publicly along with opposition for a symbolic three-and-a-half-year period. This period of God's power is followed by a period of Satan's power. Jesus was crucified. He "was dead." But, Satan's victory was short lived, because after three days, Jesus was resurrected and alive forevermore. The two witnesses also were killed, and their enemies rejoiced. But now severe persecution by Satan has been reduced to three-and-a-half symbolic days! Christians who were "in the tribulation" were comforted with the knowledge that the persecution would not last for a long time. When compared to the time of evangelism, the period of severe suffering will be short. This is the message of ***the little book***.

***In the same hour there was a great earthquake, and a tenth of the city fell. In the earthquake seven thousand people were killed.* 11:13** ^{NKJV} An earthquake is a symbol for God's judgment. The tenth of the city and the seven thousand indicate that this is partial judgment like the first six trumpets. The final Day of Judgment is reserved for the seventh trumpet. The city in the vision is Jerusalem, but it represents the wicked world because "it has been given over to the Gentiles." (11:2)

***And the rest were afraid and gave glory to the God of heaven.* 11:13** NKJV The first six trumpets had not sounded in vain. Although the majority would not repent (9:20-21), a minority remnant heard the trumpets and repented of their sins. To fear and give glory to God is to express repentance and worship.[58] Unbelievers became converts as they witnessed the way Christians faced and survived ten severe persecutions by the Romans. The church continued to grow even though it was persecuted by the Roman Empire.[59] Christ is riding the white horse to victory along with the red, black, and pale horses!

***The second woe is past; and, behold, the third woe comes quickly.* 11:14** This is a transitional statement, reminding us that the sixth trumpet has sounded. There has been an interlude between the sixth and the seventh trumpets. (10:1 - 11:13) The purpose is to assure the church of its victory and salvation. There was space between the sixth and seventh seals for the same reason in Revelation 7. The seventh trumpet is the third woe.

The Seventh Trumpet

***The seventh angel sounded his trumpet, and there were loud voices in heaven, which said, "The kingdom of the world has become the kingdom of our Lord and of his Christ; and he will reign for ever and ever." * 11:15** NIV Daniel had predicted that the kingdom of God "shall break in pieces and consume all these kingdoms, and it

---

[58] Revelation 14:7 and Revelation 15:4
[59] F. W. Mattox, *The Eternal Kingdom*, p. 98

shall stand forever." (Daniel 2:44) The kingdoms of this world may persecute the saints of God, but these kingdoms will rise and fall. (Daniel 2:20-21) Christians have an eternal kingdom that will be victorious over all the earthly kingdoms.

And the twenty-four elders who were seated on their thrones before God, fell on their faces and worshiped God, saying: "We give thanks to you, Lord God Almighty, the One, who is and who was, because you have taken your great power and have begun to reign." **11:16-17** [NIV] The leaders of the redeemed of both the Old and New Testaments give reverence and grateful praise to the eternal God who has conquered all of his enemies.

"And the nations were angry, and your wrath is come, and the time of the dead, that they should be judged, and that you should give reward to your servants the prophets, and to the saints, and them that fear your name, small and great; and should destroy them which destroy the earth." **11:18** This describes the Judgment at the end of time. God's faithful servants will receive their reward at the same time the wicked are judged and punished. (John 5:28-29; Matthew 25:31-46)

Then God's temple in heaven was opened, and within his temple was seen the ark of his covenant. And there came flashes of lightning, rumblings, peals of thunder, an earthquake and a great hailstorm. **11:19** [NIV] This is a symbolic vision. John saw no temple in the heavenly city, the New Jerusalem, because the Lord God and Christ are its temple. (21:22) The temple with the ark of the covenant, the golden altar of incense, the golden lampstand, and the harps were all symbols. The ark of God's covenant symbolizes atonement. The lightning, thunder, earthquake, and hail symbolize God's presence and wrath. (Ex. 19:16-18) Acceptable worship to God is "with reverence and godly fear." (Heb. 12:28)

On the Day of Judgment, those redeemed by the blood of the Lamb will be able to enter the temple opened in heaven—they will have fellowship with God. Those who are denied entrance will suffer the wrath of God.

The seventh trumpet describes the end of time, but we are only half way through the book of Revelation. This is proof that Revelation contains parallelism—seven parallel views of the victorious church.

The key in chapter one, verse eighteen has been used and demonstrated throughout the first half of the book. The church will be like its Lord and Savior Jesus Christ, who said, *"I am he who lives, and was dead, and behold, I am alive forevermore."* There will be long periods of evangelism, that are followed by short periods of severe persecution, and then victory for the church. The church will share with Jesus in his earthly ministry, his death and resurrection. This cycle occurs again and again throughout the Christian age until the seventh trumpet sounds and Christ comes for the great and final Day of Judgment. This is the reason that so many specific interpretations of the symbols of Revelation seem to fit so many different persons, places, and times.

Review Questions on Lesson 6

1. The mighty angel with one foot on the sea and the other on the land symbolizes the _____ of God.

2. The little book's message is that there will be a cycle of sweet (_____) and bitter (_____).

3. John was told to measure the _____ that included only the _____ _____ and the _____ _____ _____.

4. What does *measuring* symbolize? _____

5. What was not to be measured? Why?
   _____
   _____

6. The 42 months for Jerusalem to be trodden under foot by the Gentiles and the 1,260 days for the two witnesses to prophesy equal how many years? _____

7. God gave _____ to his witnesses for 1,260 days.

8. How did God show his power during the time of Elijah?
   _____

9. How did Satan imitate God's power in 168 - 165 BC?
   _____

10. How many years did God demonstrate his power during the ministry of Jesus? _____

11. God's two witnesses represent the _____ of the church.

12. The two witnesses were _____ by the beast that came up from the bottomless pit.

13. Jerusalem is now called *Sodom* and *Egypt* to symbolize its _____ and _____.

14. The two witnesses were dead for how long? _____

15. What caused "great fear" to fall on the people?
    _____

16. When the seventh trumpet sounded, the time had come for the dead to be _____.

17. What was opened in heaven? _____

18. The seventh trumpet describes the _____ of time.

View 4

The Victorious Lamb

Revelation 12 – 14

NOTES

The Woman & the Dragon
Revelation 12

Revelation 12 is about the church surviving two great persecutions by Roman emperors during the first century. The first was by **Nero** from AD 64 to 68. The second was by **Domitian** from 95 to 96. The book of Revelation was written at this time. The early church historian Eusebius wrote: "With terrible cruelty, Domitian ... showed himself Nero's successor in hostility to God. He was the second to organize a persecution against us, though his father, Vespasian, had no such evil plans."[60] In Revelation 12, there is a long period of evangelism, followed by a short period of persecution. Then there is another long time of evangelism, followed by a second severe persecution against the church. This cycle can be seen in church history.

And there appeared a great wonder in heaven: a woman clothed with the sun, with the moon under her feet, and upon her head a crown of twelve stars. **12:1** This glorious woman is spiritual Israel, God's holy nation, as indicated by the twelve stars that form a victor's wreath. God spoke to Israel at Mount Sinai, "Now therefore, if you will indeed obey My voice and keep My covenant, then you shall be a special treasure to Me above all people...and you shall be to Me a kingdom of priests and a holy nation." (Exodus 19:5-6) NKJV In the New Testament, Peter writes similar words to the church, "But you are a chosen generation, a royal priesthood, a holy nation, His own special people." (1 Peter 2:9) NKJV God's holy nation today is his victorious church! The number *twelve* symbolizes God's people. There were twelve tribes of Israel and twelve apostles. (21:12-14)

---

[60] Paul L. Maier, *Eusebius—The Church History*, p. 104

The ***twelve stars*** of the victor's crown represent the angels that are watching over, protecting, and serving the people of God. (1:20; Hebrews 1:13-14) Spiritual Israel is ***clothed with the sun***. The Christ would be called "the Sun of Righteousness" according to Malachi 4:2. Jesus said, "I am the light of the world" in John 8:12. Spiritual Israel today is composed of Christians, who are clothed with Christ and with his righteousness. "For all of you who were baptized into Christ have clothed yourselves with Christ." (Galatians 3:27) NIV ***"The moon under her feet"*** is showing that Christ and his church will be victorious over all enemies as the sun outshines the moon. (17:14)

And the woman ***being with child cried, travailing in birth. 12:2*** In verse five, it is clear that the child is Christ, who came from Israel. (Romans 9:4-5) God carried out his plan to bring the Savior into the world through the faithful remnant of Israel. (Rom. 11:5, 13-27) The woman is **spiritual** Israel, not fleshly Israel, "for they are not all Israel, which are of Israel." (Rom. 9:6)

And there appeared another wonder in heaven: and behold, a great red dragon having seven heads and ten horns, and seven crowns on his heads. 12:3 Verse nine tells us the dragon is Satan. His destructiveness is indicated by his fiery red color. The seven crowns on his seven heads are diadems of usurped power that represent his influence upon the rulers of the world that persecute God's people. (13:1-2) Jesus called Satan "the prince of this world" in John 12:31. The ten horns symbolize ten Roman emperors that would persecute the church. (17:12-14) ***His tail drew the third part of the stars of heaven and did cast them to the earth. 12:4*** The ***stars*** symbolize angels. (1:20) This refers to "the angels who did not stay within their own positions of authority" but joined Satan's rebellion against God. (Jude 6) ESV

And the dragon stood before the woman which was ready to be delivered, for to devour her child as soon as it was born. **12:4** Satan through the wicked king Herod tried to kill Jesus when he was born. (Matthew 2:1-20)

The woman gave birth to a male child. And her son *was to rule all nations with a rod of iron.* **12:5** The Christ was to rule all nations with a rod of iron, according to Psalm 2:8-9.

And her child was caught up unto God and to his throne. **12:5** When Satan tried to destroy him through temptations, Jesus defeated him with the written word of God. (Luke 4:1-13) He "was in all points tempted like as we are, yet without sin." (Hebrews 4:15) Beginning at his hometown of Nazareth, several attempts were made to kill Jesus, but God protected him during his ministry of three-and-a-half years.[61] When Jesus was on the cross, it appeared that Satan had been successful in his attempt to destroy him. However, three days later Jesus Christ was "declared to be the Son of God with power ... by the resurrection from the dead." (Romans 1:4) Christ victoriously ascended through the clouds to God's throne in heaven to begin reigning over the kingdom of God. (Acts 1:1-11, Acts 2:32-36, Daniel 7:13-14)

And the woman fled into the wilderness, where she has a place prepared of God that they should feed her there a thousand two hundred and sixty days. **12:6** Israel went into the wilderness and received bread from heaven after being saved from the Egyptians at the Red Sea.[62] The church is the place prepared by God for his people, spiritual Israel. (Ephesians 3:10-21) God's people are fed spiritually with his word. (John 6:35, 63)

---

[61] Luke 4:16-30; John 5:16-18; John 8:59; John 10:31
[62] Exodus 14:27; Exodus 16:1-4; 1 Corinthians 10:1-6

This takes place during the one ***thousand two hundred and sixty days*** when the two witnesses are able to preach. (11:3-6) This period is the same length of time as the three-and-a-half years of Jesus' earthly ministry and is symbolic of any period in which the church is able to preach and worship without severe persecution. For over thirty years, the church was not persecuted by the Roman government—from its beginning on Pentecost until Nero's persecution that began in AD 64. In fact, the Romans protected Christians.[63]

And there was war in heaven: Michael and his angels fought against the dragon; and the dragon and his angels fought and prevailed not, neither was their place found any more in heaven. **12:7-8** This is describing the spiritual conflict that began when Satan and his angels rebelled against God. (Jude 6)[64] Michael, an archangel of God, watches over and defends God's people. (Jude 9; Daniel 12:1) During his earthly ministry, Jesus said, "I beheld Satan as lightning fall from heaven" (Luke 10:18), and "now shall the prince of this world be cast out." (John 12:31) This is symbolic language. Satan can no longer stand before God as an accuser of the brethren. By shedding his blood for our sins, Jesus dealt a crushing blow to the head of Satan. (Genesis 3:15) "Who shall bring a charge against God's elect? It is God who justifies. Who is he who condemns? It is Christ who died, and furthermore is also risen, who is even at the right hand of God, who also makes intercession for us." (Romans 8:33-34) NKJV

And the great dragon was cast out, that old serpent, called the Devil and Satan, which deceives the whole world; he was cast out into the earth, and his angels were cast out with him. **12:9** The serpent that tempted

---

[63] Acts 18:12-16; Acts 19:28-41; Acts 21:30-32; Acts 23:12-35
[64] Daniel 10:5-21

and deceived mother Eve is clearly identified as Satan, the Devil. (Genesis 3:1-13) His name is **Satan**, which describes him as our adversary or enemy. He is called *the Devil*, which means the accuser and slanderer.

Then John heard a loud voice in heaven saying, "Now is come salvation and strength and the kingdom of our God and the power of his Christ for the accuser of our brethren is cast down, which accused them before our God day and night. And they overcame him by the blood of the Lamb and by the word of their testimony; and they loved not their lives unto death."
12:10-11 Salvation came when Christ died on the cross. By shedding his blood, he defeated Satan and cast him down. Jesus has made us free from the slavery of sin. (John 8:31-36) When salvation came, so did the kingdom of God. The Father "has delivered us from the power of darkness and has translated us into the kingdom of his dear Son, in whom we have redemption through his blood, even the forgiveness of sins." (Colossians 1:13-14) To overcome Satan, one must be willing to confess Christ not only with his mouth but also with his life even to death. (Matt. 10:32; Matt. 16:24-25; Rev. 2:10)

Therefore rejoice you heavens and you that dwell in them. Woe to the inhabiters of the earth and of the sea! For the devil is come down unto you, having great wrath, because he knows that he has but a short time.
12:12 The devil has been defeated. Jesus has demonstrated his power over the devil by his sacrifice for our sins and his victorious resurrection from the dead. However, Satan still has power to tempt, deceive, and harm men. "Your adversary the devil, as a roaring lion, walks about, seeking whom he may devour." (1 Peter 5:8) Satan has great wrath. He now seeks to destroy the church, but his time to persecute Christians has been limited to *a short time.*

***And when the dragon saw that he had been cast unto the earth, he persecuted the woman which brought forth the man child.* 12:13** This persecution against the church was the one by Nero. It was for a **short time** and corresponded to the time when Jesus **was dead.** (1:18) It was for the same time that the two witnesses were dead figuratively for three-and-a-half days. (Rev. 11:7-11)

***And to the woman were given two wings of a great eagle that she might fly into the wilderness into her place, where she is nourished for a time, and times, and half a time, from the face of the serpent.* 12:14** God's protection is being emphasized. With similar words, God encouraged Israel in Exodus 19:4, "You have seen what I did unto the Egyptians, and how I bore you on eagles' wings and brought you unto myself." This was a demonstration of God's power. The wilderness was a place of refuge and protection. God fed his people with manna from heaven. Today, God's people are nourished with the Bread of Life, our Lord Jesus Christ, when the church is able to teach and preach his word. (John 6:27, 48, 63) The **time and times and a half time** refer to the same period that is in verse six, when the woman is being fed in the wilderness for **one thousand, two hundred and sixty days**. This is the symbolic three-and-a-half years of evangelism. Following the death of the Roman emperor Nero in AD 68, the church enjoyed a long period without severe persecution. Nero's successors, Vespasian and Titus, did not persecute Christians. "Under the rule of Vespasian (69-79) there was no record of Christians suffering for their faith."[65] During this time, the church was avenged by God over the unbelieving Jews who were the first to persecute it. God allowed the Romans to destroy Jerusalem in AD 70. The church was victorious over the Jewish nation that had sought to destroy it!

---

[65] F. W. Mattox, *The Eternal Kingdom*, p. 93

***And the serpent cast out of his mouth water as a flood after the woman, that he might cause her to be carried away of the flood. And the earth helped the woman, and the earth opened her mouth and swallowed up the flood which the dragon cast out of his mouth.* 12:15-16** Just as the Jews were unsuccessful for three-and-a-half years in several attempts to kill Jesus during his ministry, Satan will not be able to silence the church during its long period of evangelism. In his special providence, God protected the church from AD 68 to 95.

And the dragon was enraged with the woman, and he went to make war with the rest of her offspring, who keep the commandments of God and have the testimony of Jesus Christ.* 12:17** ^{NKJV} Domitian the Roman emperor began his persecution against the church in AD 95. Those that were "born again" by the proclamation of the gospel were ***her offspring. John called his converts "my children" in 3 John 4. Whenever Satan and his helpers make ***war*** against the church, a severe persecution is meant. John and his fellow Christians were suffering in this tribulation. (1:9) It would be for just ***a little while.*** (6:9-11) In fact, it lasted one year. In AD 96, Domitian was killed by a man that he trusted.

Daniel had predicted that Domitian's persecution of "the saints" would be "for a time and times and half a time." (Daniel 7:23-25) A ***time*** may refer to a year, but not always. Keil & Delitzsch state that in Daniel 7:25 the ***times*** are not years.[66] Barnes says that the word translated ***time*** may refer to a day, a month, a year, or any other measure of duration.[67] The persecution by Domitian lasted only a year—not three and a half years. The time is symbolic. What then is the meaning of Daniel's prophecy? If we take the ***time*** to be a ***day***, it

---

[66] Keil & Delitzsch, *Commentary of the Old Testament*, Daniel 4:16
[67] Albert Barnes, *Barnes Notes on The Old Testament,* Daniel 4:16

would agree with Revelation 11:11, where the two witnesses are dead for only three-and-a-half days. Satan's time of power has been reduced from three-and-a-half years in the time of Antiochus IV to three-and-a-half symbolic days. Christians will be silenced and suffer severely for only a short time in comparison to the time that they are able to teach and preach. John and his fellow Christians would have been greatly encouraged by this message.

Summary of Events in Revelation 12

Christ's Ministry	Church's Ministry symbolic 1,260 days	Church's Ministry time, times, ½ time
3 ½ years	31 years	27 years
dead	dead	dead
3 days	"short time"	"the tribulation"
	Nero	Domitian
AD 33	64-68	95-96

Review Questions on Lesson 7

1. Revelation 12 is about the church surviving persecutions by two Roman emperors, _____ and _____.

2. Who is the woman in Revelation 12?
   _____

3. What are the twelve stars symbolizing?
   _____

4. The woman is clothed with the _____ representing Christ and his_____.

5. What does the moon under her feet symbolize?
   _____
   _____

6. Who stood before the woman waiting to devour her child as soon as he was born? _____

7. What is the great fiery red dragon called in Rev. 12:9?
   _____

8. The dragon had _____ heads and _____ horns.

9. What did the dragon have on his heads?
   _____

10. What is symbolized by the dragon's tail drawing a third of the stars of heaven and throwing them to the earth?
    _____

11. Who is the male child of the woman? _____

12. How was the male child delivered from the dragon? v. 5
    _____

13. The woman fled into what place? 12:6
    _____

14. There the woman was fed for how many days?
    _____

15. What were the two witnesses able to do in the same number of days? 11:3-6 _____

16. Who fought a war in heaven against the dragon and his angels? _____

17. When salvation came, the _____ also came.

18. How did the brethren overcome and conquer the dragon?
    _____

19. Why does the dragon, the devil, have great wrath? 12:12
    _____

20. Whom did the dragon persecute when he saw he had been cast down to the earth? _____

21. This first persecution was by Roman Emperor _____.

22. The woman was given two wings of a great eagle so she could return to her place in the wilderness, where she was nourished for how long? _____

23. How is the woman protected during this time? _____
    _____

24. After the 2nd period of protection, with whom did the dragon make war? _____

25. This second Roman persecution was by _____.

26. The time that the woman is fed and nourished and the time the two witnesses in chapter eleven are able to preach are equal to the time of the _____ of Jesus on the earth.

The Two Beasts & The Lamb
Revelation 13 – 14

The dragon, symbolizing Satan, was persecuting Christ and his church in chapter twelve. Now we see two beasts representing the wicked rulers and religious leaders that Satan uses to carry out his persecutions. However, Christ the Lamb will be victorious over these two beasts and those that follow them.

The Two Beasts

In the closing verse of chapter twelve, the dragon went out "to make war" against Christians, describing the second Roman persecution against the church, AD 95-96, by Emperor Domitian. The earlier and better manuscripts read, ***The dragon stood on the shore of the sea.*** **13:1** ^{NIV} The dragon stood on the sand of the seashore to call forth one of his agents of persecution.

Then John *saw a beast rise up out of the sea, having seven heads and ten horns, and upon his horns ten crowns, and upon his heads the name of blasphemy. And the beast which I saw was like a leopard, and his feet were as the feet of a bear, and his mouth as the mouth of a lion: and the dragon gave him his power, and his seat, and great authority.* **13:1-2** The *sea* represents the ungodly masses of peoples and nations in their restless condition. (17:15) The beast that John saw coming up out of the sea was a combination of the four beasts coming up out of the sea in the vision of Daniel 7:2-8. In Daniel's vision, the four beasts represent four kingdoms. The **lion** is the Babylonian Empire. The **bear** symbolizes the kingdom of the Medes and Persians. Alexander the Great and the Greeks are represented by a **leopard.** A beast with **ten horns** is the fourth kingdom, the Roman Empire. (Daniel 7:17, 23)

Each of the seven heads of the beast that John saw had a mouth like the *lion*. His feet were like the *bear*. His body was like the *leopard*. And one of the heads had *ten horns* like Daniel's *fourth beast*, the Roman Empire. The *ten crowns* on the ten horns are diadems of Satan's power. The beast has *seven heads*, representing all rulers that blaspheme God and persecute his people. Each head has a blasphemous name. These seven heads are connected to the one beast. (17:9-11) Although they represent various nations at different times and places, they all belong to the beast. All rulers that try to destroy God's people are serving as instruments of Satan.

John *saw one of his heads as it was wounded to death, and his deadly wound was healed.* **13:3** The seven heads represent seven kings or kingdoms. (17:9-10) The head that came back to life and was persecuting Christians belonged to the Roman Empire. Satan was imitating Christ's death and resurrection. When Nero died in AD 68, the persecution of Christians by the Romans appeared to be over, but it was revived by Domitian in AD 95. The early church historian Eusebius testified that "Domitian showed himself Nero's successor in hostility to God."[68]

And the whole world was amazed and followed after the beast; and they worshiped the dragon, because he gave his authority to the beast; and they worshiped the beast, saying, "Who is like the beast, and who is able to wage war with him?" **13:3-4** ᴺᴬˢᴮ The glory and power of the Roman Empire was impressive. The inhabitants of the world were enjoying peace and prosperity. They showed their appreciation to Rome by erecting magnificent temples to the Roman emperors and worshiping them as gods. They believed that the Roman Empire would last forever. Domitian demanded to be

---

[68] Paul L. Maier, *Eusebius—The Church History*, p. 107

worshiped as "Our Master and Our God."[69] When the people worshiped the emperor, they actually were worshiping Satan, because the beast received his authority from the dragon.

And there was given to him a mouth speaking great things and blasphemies, and power was given to him to continue forty and two months. And he opened his mouth in blasphemy against God, to blaspheme his name, and his tabernacle, and them that dwell in heaven. **13:5-6** The beast was given power, but his power was limited to blasphemy for forty-two months. The Roman Emperor Domitian was the beast at the time of the Revelation. During the first fourteen years of his reign, he and the Romans showed contempt for Christians because they would not take part in the pagan festivals. Christians "were derided as haters of the human race."[70] When Christians were insulted and reviled, the Romans were showing a lack of reverence for God. Blasphemy also includes the act of claiming deity for oneself, as was done by Domitian. The beast speaks evil of God, his name (or nature), his tabernacle (heaven), and those that dwell in heaven. In his prophecy of the Roman Empire, Daniel predicted that the eleventh Roman king, Domitian, would "speak pompous words against the Most High." (Daniel 7:23-25)[NKJV] Remember that Jesus also was reviled and blasphemed during his earthly ministry for three-and-a-half years, but Satan was limited in his power to harm him.

And it was given to him to make war with the saints and to overcome them. **13:7** In the last year of his reign, Domitian was allowed to severely persecute Christians. Remember the saints suffer great tribulation when the dragon and the beast *make war* against them. However, it

---

[69] Suetonius, *Lives of the Twelve Caesars* (Suetonius, a Roman historian)
[70] Kenneth Scott Latourette, *A History of Christianity*, p. 82

is limited to **a short time** of only "three-and-a-half" figurative days. (11:7-11) The beast "was given" a mouth to blaspheme and authority to rule and to make war. Although the dragon gave him his power, his throne, and his authority (13:2), God limits and controls the activities of Satan. (9:1-5) God allowed the beast to have this power. Joe Jones states, "God has his own purposes in permitting this persecution, just as he did in the crucifixion of Jesus. God allows Satan, and therefore Rome, limited power for a limited time. All things are still under God's control."[71] Jesus said to the Roman governor Pilate, "You could have no power at all against me, except it were given you from above." (John 19:11)

And power was given him over all kindreds, and tongues, and nations. And all that dwell upon the earth shall worship him, whose names are not written in the book of life of the Lamb slain from the foundation of the world. **13:7-8** The Roman Empire ruled over all the nations surrounding the great Mediterranean Sea, most of Europe to the north, and to the east as far as the city of Babylon. The Roman emperor was worshiped as a god by the unsaved masses of the world. The Book of Life contains the names of all those that have been saved by the blood of our Lord. The death of Christ was in God's eternal purpose from the beginning of the world. (Genesis 3:9; Ephesians 3:11)

If any man has an ear, let him hear. **13:9** Special attention needs to be given to what is about to be said.

He that leads into captivity shall go into captivity; he that kills with the sword must be killed with the sword. Here is the patience and the faith of the saints. **13:10** Christians are not to take vengeance, but they are to overcome evil with good, according to Romans 12:19.

---

[71] Joe D. Jones, *Victory in Jesus*, p. 200

John and his brethren were "in tribulation and in the kingdom and patience of Jesus Christ." (1:9) God would repay in kind the persecuting Roman emperors. Within the year, Domitian would be killed, being stabbed to death by a man whom he trusted.[72] Our Lord Jesus Christ is "the ruler over the kings of the earth." (1:5) NKJV Having faith that the Lord would conquer and judge their enemies gave patience and perseverance to Christians.

John then saw *another beast coming up out of the earth; and he had two horns like a lamb, and he spoke like a dragon.* **13:11** The second beast looks like a lamb, but speaks like the Devil. Again, Satan is imitating Christ, the Lamb of God. Later, this beast from the earth is called "the false prophet" in Revelation 19:20. In general, he represents all false religions. However, these early Christians recognized the second beast as the officials who were in charge of the state religion that was promoting the worship of the Roman emperor.

And he exercises all the power of the first beast before him, and causes the earth and them which dwell therein to worship the first beast whose deadly wound was healed. **13:12** The second beast receives his authority from the persecuting government, which at that time was the Roman Empire under the rule of Domitian. The government was promoting emperor worship as proof of one's loyalty to Rome.

The second beast *does great wonders, so that he makes fire come down from heaven on the earth in the sight of men. And he deceives them that dwell on the earth by the means of those miracles which he had power to do in the sight of the beast, saying to them that dwell on the earth that they should make an image to the beast which had the wound by a sword and did live.* **13:13-14**

---

[72] Suetonius, *Lives of the Twelve Caesars, Life of Domitian*, chapter 17

Satan has power, and at times God grants permission for him to use his power. Jesus warned us in Matthew 24:24 of "false prophets" that "show great signs and wonders" in order to deceive us. Paul also warned us of "the working of Satan with all power and signs and lying wonders" in 2 Thessalonians 2:9. The purpose of his miracles and tricks at that time was to get men to worship the image of the emperor. Today, false teachers perform what they call "miracles" to convince us that they are messengers from God. Although we may not be able explain these wonders, we should not immediately conclude that these teachers have the power of God. These "great signs" may be the power of Satan or a trick. Even magicians do marvelous things that we do not understand, but they freely admit that these are tricks. John wrote, "Beloved, believe not every spirit, but try the spirits, whether they are of God; because many false prophets have gone out into the world." (1 John 4:1) We are to study the Bible, "proving what is acceptable to the Lord." (Ephesians 5:10)

And he had power to give life to the image of the beast, that the image of the beast should both speak and cause that as many as would not worship the image of the beast should be killed. 13:15 J. W. Roberts suggests that the power to make the image speak may be a reference "to ventriloquism or to the device, the means of which have been discovered by modern archaeologists, of piping the human voice beneath the altars bearing the statues of the gods."[73] Worshiping the image of the emperor was considered an act of patriotism. Christians who would not worship the image of Domitian and other Roman emperors were accused of treason, and many were killed.

---

[73] J. W. Roberts, *The Revelation to John*, p. 114

Revelation 13-14 | 111

And he causes all, both small and great, rich and poor, free and bond, to receive a mark in their right hand or in their foreheads, and that no man might buy or sell, save he that had the mark or the name of the beast, or the number of his name. **13:16-17** Because a person refused to worship the Roman emperor, he was denied the opportunity to buy or sell in the marketplace. Archaeologists have discovered certificates, which the emperor worshipers received and used as proof of having worshiped at the emperor's altar.[74] The mark of the beast is not a literal stamp or brand on the hand or forehead. Just as those who belong to God have the seal of God on their foreheads (7:3), so those who belong to Satan have the "mark of the beast." The language is symbolic in both cases. A person shows by what he does (the mark on his right hand) or even by what he thinks (the mark on his forehead) that he belongs to the beast and to the dragon (Satan).

This calls for wisdom: let the one who has understanding calculate the number of the beast, for it is the number of a man, and his number is 666. **13:18** ESV Various attempts have been made to explain this number. Irenaeus said that "666" was the sum total of the numerical values of the letters in the word **Lateinos**, the Latin man, being a reference to the Romans.[75] Perhaps the best explanation is that "666" is ***man's number*** as in the NIV. The Greek has no indefinite article, so the translation may be "it is the number of a man" or "it is the number of man." Man, who was created on the sixth day, is always falling short of perfection, just as the number "6" is always one short of the perfect number "7". Man, by himself, is striving but failing again and again and again, so his number is "666".[76] Seven is the number

---

[74] David L. Roper, *Truth for Today Commentary, Revelation 12-22*, p. 67
[75] Frank Pack, *Revelation, Part 2*, p. 11
[76] W. Hendriksen, *More Than Conquerors*, p. 182

used many times in the book of Revelation indicating perfection. Thus, the readers are reminded that the number of the beast, 666, is the number of a man, not of a god. Secular humanism, the philosophy of the Greeks and Romans, deifies man as "the measure of all things." The number "666" may symbolize secular humanism that has caused Christians to suffer persecutions. First century readers understood that "666" was referring to the worship of Roman emperors. They were men – not gods!

We know that "666" has no reference to any modern invention or to a certain Antichrist yet to come, because John told his first century readers that they could understand the meaning of the number "666".

The Victorious Lamb

***Then I looked, and there before me was the Lamb, standing on Mount Zion, and with him 144,000 who had his name and his Father's name written on their foreheads.* 14:1**[NIV] This vision reveals the victorious church with Christ in heaven—its ultimate destiny. Jesus is the true Lamb in contrast with the false lamb, the beast from the earth. (13:11-17)) The best Greek text has the definite article, "*the* Lamb." "Behold the Lamb of God who takes away the sin of the world." (John 1:29) True worship triumphs over false religion!

Mount Zion is Jerusalem, the city of David.[77] In Isaiah's prophecy predicting the establishment of the church, Zion is the city of Jerusalem. "For out of Zion shall go forth the law, and the word of the Lord from Jerusalem." (Isaiah 2:3) In Hebrews 12:22, Mount Zion symbolizes heaven. "You are come to Mount Zion, and to the city of the living God, the heavenly Jerusalem." When God speaks from Mount Zion, he "speaks from

---

[77] 2 Samuel 5:7

heaven." (Hebrews 12:22-25) Those who are standing on Mount Zion are before the throne of God (14:3), and God's throne is in heaven. (4:2)

The 144,000 are mentioned first in Revelation 7:1-8. Twelve is a symbolic number for God's people. The twelve tribes of Israel symbolize those who are faithful to God from all the tribes (or nations) of the earth. Twelve times twelve equals 144. The tabernacle in the Old Testament is a source of many symbols in Revelation. (See notes on Revelation 4:5-8.) The Most Holy Place represented God's dwelling place, his presence and glory. (Hebrews 9:24) The Most Holy Place was a cube in shape—ten cubits long, ten cubits wide, and ten cubits high. A thousand is the product of ten times ten times ten. Heaven is described as having the same length, breadth, and height. (21:15-16) Therefore, a thousand is the symbol for heaven. That makes **the 144,000 represent God's people from all the nations who will be in heaven.** Having God's name written on their foreheads is a way of saying that they belong to him. (See notes on Revelation 7:2-4.)

And I heard a voice from heaven like the sound of many waters and like the sound of loud thunder, and the voice which I heard was like the sound of harpists playing on their harps. And they sang a new song before the throne and before the four living creatures and the elders. **14:2-3** ^{NASB} The Greek word *phone* may be translated *sound* or *voice*. Three similes are used to describe the singing of the 144,000. (1) Their singing was *like* the sound of many waters; (2) it was *like* the sound of loud thunder; and (3) it was *like* the sound of harpists playing their harps. The King James Version and the New King James Version incorrectly have John hearing the sound of harpists playing their harps, but a simile of comparison is used in the Greek. John did **not** hear harpists playing harps. The song they were singing was beautiful like the melody of harps; it was powerful in volume like thunder, and had a flowing rhythm like many waters. If you have heard thousands of voices joining together in singing songs of praise to God, you may have some understanding of what is being described.

***No one could learn the song except the 144,000 who had been redeemed from the earth.* 14:3** NIV They were singing *a new song* of salvation. During their life on earth, they had sung old songs of trials and tribulations. Now they could praise the Lord with the words of Psalm 40:2-3, "He brought me up also out of a horrible pit, out of the miry clay, and set my feet upon a rock, and established my goings. And he has put *a new song* in my mouth, even praise unto our God." Only those who had been redeemed by the Lamb could sing this song of salvation. They were singing praises before the throne of God and before the cherubim and the elders. By this we know that the 144,000 are the saved in heaven.

The 144,000 *were redeemed from the earth.* **14:3** *These were redeemed from among men.* **14:4** They represent all the saved in heaven with the Lamb, who redeemed them with his blood out of every nation. (5:9) The 144,000 are spiritual *virgins.* **14:4** A Christian is described in 2 Corinthians 11:2 "as a chaste virgin to Christ" undefiled with sin and false doctrines. In 19:7-9, we read about *the marriage* of Christ the Lamb to his bride, the church. This passage is not teaching that those who have been married will not be in heaven. Forbidding marriage is a doctrine of demons. (1 Timothy 4:1-3) "Let marriage be held in honor." (Hebrews 13:4) NASB

The 144,000 *follow the Lamb.* **14:4** Faithful disciples of Christ are not following the beast that looks like a lamb, but speaks like the Devil. They are not listening to false teachers. Those that will be in heaven will have followed Christ the Lamb in his righteousness and truth.

Revelation 13-14 | **115**

The 144,000 are the *firstfruits unto God and to the Lamb*. 14:4 They belong to God just as the firstfruits of the harvest. (Exodus 23:19) The redemption of the firstborn under the Law of Moses was said to be "as a mark on your hand or frontlets between your eyes." (Exodus 13:1-16) ᴱˢⱽ James 1:18 tells Christians, "Of his own will begat he us with the word of truth, that we should be a kind of firstfruits of his creatures."

The 144,000 are *without fault before the throne of God*. 14:5 They have been walking in the light of God's word, and the blood of Jesus Christ has been cleansing them from all sin. (1 John 1:7) With humility, they have confessed their sins, and God has forgiven them and cleansed them from all unrighteousness. (1 John 1:9)

We conclude that the 144,000 is not a literal number but a figurative number that represents all of God's faithful servants who have been redeemed from all nations. They are victorious with Christ in heaven!

The Proclamations of Three Angels

And John saw *another angel fly in the midst of heaven, having the everlasting gospel to preach to them that dwell on the earth, and to every nation.* **14:6** This verse introduces another vision. We are taken back in time to three messages proclaimed by three angels for those living on the earth. The first angel has the gospel, the good news of everlasting life, because Christ died for our sins, was buried and was raised again from the dead. (1 Cor. 15:1-4) Some good news is temporary, but the gospel of Christ is everlasting. This good news is for every nation. It is the fulfillment of the promise made to Abraham, "In your seed (Christ) shall all the nations of the earth be blessed." (Gen. 22:18; Gal. 3:16) Jesus said, "Go ye into all the world and preach the gospel to every creature. He that believes and is baptized shall be saved;

but he that believes not shall be damned." (Mark 16:15-16) Paul said, "I am not ashamed of the gospel of Christ, for it is the power of God unto salvation to everyone that believes." (Romans 1:16) The first angel is warning men of God's judgment and calling sinners to repentance. He was saying, *"Fear God, and give glory to him; for the hour of his judgment is come; and worship him that made heaven, and the earth, and the sea, and the fountains of waters."* **14:7**

And there followed another angel, saying, "Babylon is fallen, is fallen, that great city, because she has made all nations drink of the wine of the wrath of her fornication" **14:8** The symbol of "Babylon" is here introduced for the first time. It represents Rome and all other ungodly cities of the world. It stands for "the lust of the flesh, and the lust of the eyes, and the pride of life." (1 John 2:16) The wine of her fornication represents all kinds of sins and immoralities that lead to God's wrath being poured out upon them. More about Babylon and its fall will be revealed in Revelation 17-19.

And a third angel followed them, saying with a loud voice, "If any man worships the beast and his image, and receives his mark on his forehead or on his hand, the same shall drink of the wine of the wrath of God, which is poured out without mixture into the cup of his indignation; and he shall be tormented with fire and brimstone in the presence of the holy angels and in the presence of the Lamb. And the smoke of their torment ascends up forever and ever; and they have no rest day or night, who worship the beast and his image, and whosoever receives the mark of his name." **14:9-11** The mark of the beast is not a literal brand. A person shows by what he thinks and by what he does that he belongs to the beast. A certificate was given to those that worshiped the Roman emperor, and then they could buy and sell in the marketplace. (13:16-17) Christians who would not worship the emperor were denied the right to buy and sell. Some were made a public spectacle and were tortured and put to death. Even today a person may get ahead financially and socially by compromising his faith. However, this advantage does not last. Things will be reversed on the Day of Judgment. Those that have the mark of the beast will receive the full measure of God's wrath. God's judgments on earth are mixed with his mercy. "He makes his sun to rise on the evil and on the good and sends rain on the just and on the unjust." (Matthew 5:45) Wine in Bible times usually was diluted with water. Those that belong to the beast will have to drink the wine of God's wrath undiluted. They will receive their sentence in the presence of Christ the Lamb, who will say, "Depart from me you cursed, into everlasting fire, prepared for the devil and his angels." (Matt. 25:41) The smoke of their torment ascends up forever, showing that their punishment is everlasting. Jesus said, "And these shall go away into everlasting punishment, but the righteous into life eternal." (Matthew 25:46)

Here is the patience of the saints: here are they that keep the commandments of God and the faith of Jesus. 14:12 Christians are reassured again of their ultimate victory. Their faith is in their Lord Jesus Christ, and they show that faith by obeying God's commandments. They are called *saints* because they have been sanctified by the sacrifice of Jesus. (Hebrews 10:10) They have been set apart for the Lord's service. (1 Cor. 6:11, 20) Therefore, they are devoted to Christ. They have patience, steadfastness and perseverance, even during severe persecution because they know that in the end Christ and his church will be victorious!

John then heard a voice from heaven saying to him, **"Write, Blessed are the dead which die in the Lord from henceforth." 14:13** There are seven beatitudes in the book of Revelation, and this is the second one. The seven are in 1:3, 14:13, 16:15, 19:9, 20:6, 22:7, and 22:14. Those who die in the Lord are blessed, because they have eternal life in Christ the Son. (1 John 5:11) They will receive "a crown of life" because they have been faithful to the Lord. (2:10)

"Yes," says the Spirit, "that they may rest from their labors, and their works follow them." **14:13** NKJV The Holy Spirit adds an "amen" to this beatitude. He says, "Yes." He then explains the nature of the blessing. In contrast to the wicked and unfaithful, who "have no rest" (v. 11), those who die in the Lord have *rest.* They *rest* from their hardships and persecutions. However, they are still active, for they serve God day and night before his throne. (7:14-15) The Greek word translated *rest* also has the meaning of *being refreshed*.[78] Their works will be remembered on the Judgment Day. (2 Corinthians 5:10; Matthew 25:31-40)

Then John looked, and he saw *a white cloud, and upon the cloud one sat like the Son of Man, having on his head a golden crown, and in his hand a sharp sickle.* **14:14** Jesus Christ the Son of Man was sitting on a white cloud, representing God's pure and fair judgment. Jesus is coming with clouds. (1:7; Matthew 26:64) On his head was a golden crown of victory! The sharp sickle symbolizes the time of harvest and judgment. (Joel 3:13)

And another angel came out of the temple, crying with a loud voice to him that sat on the cloud, "Thrust in your sickle and reap, for the time is come for you to reap, for the harvest of the earth is ripe." And he that sat on the cloud thrust in his sickle on the earth, and the earth was reaped. **14:15-16** Jesus said that only God the Father knows when the earth will pass away. (Matthew 24:35-36) The angel came out of the temple carrying the message

---

[78] Joseph H. Thayer, *Greek-English Lexicon of the New Testament,* p. 40

from God the Father that the time had come for Christ to reap the entire earth. Jesus said, "The harvest is the end of the world, and the reapers are the angels." (Matthew 13:39) Faithful Christians are the ripe harvest of the earth's wheat that will be gathered into God's barn; that is heaven. (Matthew 13:30) When Christ comes, he will deliver the kingdom to God the Father. (1 Cor. 15:23-24) "Then the righteous will shine forth as the sun in the kingdom of their Father." (Matthew 13:43) ^{NKJV}

And another angel came out of the temple which is in heaven, he also having a sharp sickle. And another angel came out from the altar, which had power over fire, and cried with a loud cry to him who had the sharp sickle, saying, "Thrust in your sickle and gather the clusters of the vine of the earth, for her grapes are fully ripe." **14:17-18** The harvest of the grapes symbolizes God's judgment upon the wicked. The angel who came from the altar indicates that this judgment is in answer to the prayers of the saints who have suffered persecution. (6:9-11, 8:3-6) "The Son of man shall send forth his angels, and they shall gather out of his kingdom all things that offend and them which do iniquity; and shall cast them into a furnace of fire: there shall be wailing and gnashing of teeth." (Matthew 13:41-42)

And the angel thrust in his sickle into the earth and gathered the vine of the earth, and cast it into the great winepress of the wrath of God. And the winepress was trodden without the city, and blood came out of the winepress, even unto the horse bridles, by the space of one thousand and six hundred furlongs. **14:19-20** Blood came out of the winepress instead of juice. The blood of all the faithful martyrs is being avenged outside the heavenly city, the New Jerusalem. (22:14-15) The 1,600 symbolizes that the wrath of heaven (1,000) upon sinful mankind (6, man's number) is totally complete (100 which is 10 x 10). Galatians 6:7-8 warns, "Be not deceived; God is not mocked: for whatever a man sows, that shall he also reap. For he that sows to his flesh shall of the flesh reap corruption; but he that sows to the Spirit shall of the Spirit reap life everlasting."

The fourth parallel view in Revelation comes to an end with Christ and his church standing victoriously in heaven and the wicked being eternally punished.

Review Questions on Lesson 8

1. The beast from the sea had _____ heads and a body like a _____, feet like a _____, a mouth like a _____, and ten _____.

2. The *sea* represents the ungodly masses of _____ and _____ in a restless condition.

3. This beast represents all rulers that _____ God and _____ God's people.

4. The _____ gives the beast his power and throne.

5. The head that was killed and came back to life represents the persecuting rulers of the _____ Empire.

6. The power of the beast was limited to _____ for 42 months, and then he was allowed to make _____ with the saints and conquer them.

7. The beast that came up from the earth had two horns like a _____, but he spoke like the _____.

8. This second beast represents _____ _____.

9. How did the second beast deceive the people so that they would worship the first beast? _____
_____

10. What was the penalty for not worshiping the beast from the sea? _____

11. Who could buy or sell in the marketplace? 13:17 _____
_____

12. What is meant by the mark of the beast on one's forehead or hand? _____

13. Who's number is "666" in 13:18, NIV? _____

14. The Lamb was on Mount Zion with _____ that represent the _____ from the earth.

15. Did John hear harps in heaven? _____

16. The 144,000 were singing a _____ song.

17. The first angel had the eternal _____ of Christ.

18. The second angel announced the fall of _____.

19. The third angel announced that those that worship the beast will receive the full measure of God's _____.

20. Who are blessed according to Revelation 14:13?
    _____

21. The _____ was ripe for harvest and was reaped.

The Key to Revelation

Long Period Evangelism	Short Period Tribulation	Judgment & Victory
Revelation 12:6 Church is fed 1,260 days or 3 ½ years.	Revelation 12:12-13 Devil has great wrath. Nero's persecution "a short time"	Revelation 12:14 Church is given wings of eagle to victory.
Revelation 12:14-16 Church is fed 3 ½ years	Revelation 12:17 Devil makes war. Domitian's persecution Revelation 1:9 Christians are in tribulation. Revelation is being written	
Revelation 13:5 Church is blasphemed 42 months or 3 ½ years.	Revelation 13:7 The beast, Domitian, makes war against the saints for one year.	Revelation 14:1 Christ & Church are victorious! Their enemies are judged.

View 5

The Seven Bowls of Wrath

Revelation 15 – 16

NOTES

The Seven Bowls of Wrath
Revelation 15 - 16

We have seen four views of the victorious church. In the first view, chapters 1-3, Christ is encouraging, correcting, and instructing his church, which is symbolized by seven lampstands. The second view, 4-7, shows the opening of the seven seals that reveal God's plans for the future. God is on his throne in heaven. The church is preaching the gospel along with various hardships. Brief periods of severe persecution will be followed by God's judgments upon the persecutors. Ultimately, the church will be victorious in heaven. The third view, 8-11, reveals the seven trumpets that warn sinners and announce the final Day of Judgment. In the fourth view, 12-14, the dragon and two beasts try to destroy the church, but the church is victorious!

The fifth view is the seven bowls of God's wrath that are poured out upon sinners. These different views of the victorious church are parallel to each other. This may be seen when we compare the seven bowls of wrath with the seven trumpets. The trumpets warn sinners; the bowls of wrath punish sinners. God does not reserve his entire wrath for the final Judgment Day. His wrath is being revealed now when the first six bowls are poured. The present tense is used in Romans 1:18, "For the wrath of God is revealed from heaven against all ungodliness and unrighteousness of men." The same event may be punishment for some and a warning to others. God was pouring out bowls of wrath when the Egyptians were destroyed in the Red Sea and when two powerful kings of the Amorites, Sihon and Og, were defeated by the Israelites on the east side of the Jordan River. However, when Rahab and her family heard of these events, they were hearing trumpets blowing, so they turned to God for their salvation. (Joshua 2:1-11, 6:22-25) The seventh bowl is God's wrath on the final Day of Judgment as described in Romans 2:5-11.

John writes, *And I saw another sign in heaven, great and marvelous: seven angels having the seven last plagues, for in them is filled up the wrath of God.* **15:1** The seven bowls of wrath are called the last plagues. They are being compared to the ten plagues upon the Egyptians during the time of Moses, when the people of Israel were delivered from their bondage in Egypt. There are seven bowls because God's wrath is **complete** in them. This is another example of the symbolic use of the number seven. The seventh bowl parallels the seventh trumpet. When the seventh trumpet sounds, it is not only the time for God's wrath but also "the time of the dead, that they should be judged." (11:15-18) The seventh bowl is not the fall of the Roman Empire, but the final Day of Judgment when God's full wrath is poured out at the end of time!

And I saw as it were a sea of glass mingled with fire and them that had gotten the victory over the beast, and over his image, and over his mark, and over the number of his name, stand on the sea of glass, having the harps of God. **15:2** The symbolism is from Israel's victory over the Egyptians at the Red Sea. The fiery sea of glass represents God's judgment and victory over those that have persecuted his servants. God's punishment of the wicked is symbolized by fire. The word *on* can mean "in close proximity with" as in "a village *on* the sea"; so some translations have the victors standing *"beside"* the sea. The Israelites sung a song of victory after they had passed through the sea. (Ex. 15:1-19) The sea of glass before God's throne in heaven is like crystal. (4:6) The Red Sea was deliverance for Israel and destruction for the persecuting Egyptians. Crystal stands for holiness. Those who have passed through the sea have been purified by the Lord. The harps are symbols for praise as they are in Revelation 5:8.

Before revealing the wrath of God upon the wicked, his faithful servants are being reminded of their ultimate victory. In the second view, Christians were assured of their salvation in chapter seven, after the first six seals were opened. In the third view, their ultimate victory is promised just before the last trumpet sounds. (10:1 – 11:14) In the fourth view, the redeemed are standing victoriously with the Lamb in heaven on Mount Zion (14:1-5), before those that have the mark of the beast are punished. In this fifth view, they are standing by the sea of glass as the victors in heaven! (Rev. 4:6)

And they sing the song of Moses, the servant of God, and the song of the Lamb. **15:3** The song of Moses praises God for the deliverance of Israel at the Red Sea. The song of the Lamb praises God for our victory in Jesus Christ. This shows that the victory is not limited to Christians during the Roman Empire. Those beside the sea of glass represent God's victorious servants from both the Old and New Testaments, just like the twenty-four elders represent the faithful leaders of both covenants. (4:4) Christians are reminded that God has always given his servants victory over their persecutors.

The victors are singing, *"Great and marvelous are thy works, Lord God Almighty; just and true are thy ways, thou King of saints. Who shall not fear thee, O Lord, and glorify thy name? for thou only art holy: for all nations shall come and worship before thee; for thy judgments are made manifest."* **15:3-4** All nations will see God's power as he saves his people. His victories over the Egyptians, the Assyrians, the Babylonians, the Medes and Persians, and the Greeks, would assure his servants of their victory over the Roman Empire and over any future government that would persecute it.

After seeing the ultimate victory of the church in heaven, John was taken back in time to his own day when the next vision appeared. ***Behold, the temple of the tabernacle of the testimony in heaven was opened. And the seven angels came out of the temple, having the seven plagues, clothed in pure and white linen, and having their breasts girded with golden girdles.* 15:5-6** The seven angels with the seven last plagues came out of God's dwelling place. They were clothed in pure linen and golden bands representing God's holiness and his authority as they execute his wrath.

***Then one of the four living creatures gave to the seven angels seven golden bowls full of the wrath of God who lives forever and ever.* 15:7** NKJV The living creatures are cherubim that are around the throne of God. (4:6-8) One of these cherubim gave a bowl full of God's wrath to each of the seven angels whose assignment is to bring the seven last plagues upon the wicked world.

***And the temple was filled with smoke from the glory of God and from his power; and no man was able to enter into the temple till the seven plagues of the seven angels were fulfilled.* 15:8** The Lord's glory filled the tabernacle and the temple when they were dedicated, and no one was able to enter them.[79] This glory was a demonstration of God's presence and power. The smoke is a symbol of his wrath.[80] The time for repentance had past. The complete and full punishment of unbelieving sinners would come when the seventh bowl was poured out.

The statement that no man could enter the temple till the seven plagues were completed proves that the seven bowls of wrath and the seven trumpets are parallel views. The temple was closed until the seventh bowl of wrath

---

[79] Exodus 40:35 and 2 Chronicles 7:1-2
[80] Isaiah 6:4-7, Psalm 18:8-15

had been poured out. After the seventh trumpet sounded, the dead were judged and the saints were rewarded and the wicked punished. (11:15, 18) Then "the temple of God was opened in heaven." (11:19) The parallel views agree that the temple in heaven was not opened until after the seven trumpets sounded and the seven bowls of wrath were poured out. Also, this proves that the saved do not go directly into heaven at death, but are in the heavenly Paradise of Hades. (Luke 23:43, Acts 2:27)

Then John heard a loud voice from the temple saying to the seven angels, *"Go your ways and pour out the bowls of the wrath of God upon the earth."* **16:1** The first six bowls are not limited to a special time. Examples of the pouring out of God's wrath may be found in both the Old and New Testaments.[81] Bowls of God's wrath also may be seen in world history. Events in the present and future may be seen as bowls of wrath. But the seventh bowl is a one-time occurrence reserved for the final Day of Judgment.

And the first went and poured out his bowl upon the earth; and there fell a bad and grievous sore upon the men which had the mark of the beast and upon them which worshiped his image. **16:2** When the first trumpet sounded, hail and fire mingled with blood were thrown down "to the earth." (8:7) Thus, both the first trumpet and the first bowl of wrath caused plagues upon the earth. The sixth plague upon the Egyptians was boils that broke out in sores. (Ex. 9:8-11) Another example of this bowl of wrath is the death of Herod Agrippa. He had killed the apostle James and had imprisoned Peter. (Acts 12:1-4) In Acts 12:23, we read, "An angel of the Lord struck him down, and he was eaten by worms and died." ᴺᴵⱽ Some of the diseases suffered by the wicked are a direct result of their sins. (Rom. 1:27) Diseases killed great numbers of

---

[81] Nahum 1:1-6 and Acts 5:1-11 are examples

people in the Roman Empire contributing to its decline. The reduced population resulted in fewer soldiers, farmers, and taxpayers.[82] **The first bowl of wrath is diseases on the earth.**

Sicknesses suffered by righteous believers are not part of the first bowl of wrath. Job was "blameless and upright, he feared God and shunned evil." And Satan unjustly "afflicted Job with painful sores from the soles of his feet to the top of his head."[83] However, God causes even these sufferings to "work together for good" in the lives of those who love him and are living according to his purpose.[84]

And the second angel poured out his bowl upon the sea, and it became as the blood of a dead man; and every living soul in the sea died. **16:3** When the second trumpet sounded, a third of the *sea* became blood. (8:8) Both the second trumpet and the second bowl are dealing with death at sea. During the Exodus, God destroyed the Egyptian army by drowning it in the Red Sea.

In 1588, Spain attempted to invade England with a huge fleet of 130 ships called "The Invincible Armada." However, God changed the course of history with a small English navy and a great storm at sea. Although they were outnumbered, the English ships were smaller and more maneuverable. They broke up the Spanish attack, by setting old ships on fire and sending them into the formation of Spanish ships. When the Spanish began retreating, a storm arose at sea destroying and sinking many of the Spanish ships. The English called the storm the "Protestant winds." The greatly crippled Spanish armada returned home, never to be a serious threat to

---

[82] Addison-Wesley, *World History Traditions and New Directions*, p. 144
[83] Job 2:1-7 and Job 1:1, NIV
[84] Romans 8:28, Job 42:10, 2 Corinthians 12:7-9

England again.[85] That is why North America is not predominantly Roman Catholic like Central and South America. The Spanish Inquisition had been brutal in its persecution of Christians who were trying to go back to the Bible for religious authority. **The second bowl of wrath is calamities at sea.**

And the third angel poured out his bowl upon the rivers and fountains of waters, and they became blood. **16:4** Again we see the similarity of the bowls and the trumpets. When the third trumpet sounded, rivers and springs of water became polluted, and many men died. (8:10-11) The first plague upon the Egyptians was water turned into blood. (Exodus 7:17-25)

When God used the Babylonians in 586 BC to destroy the city of Jerusalem because of its idolatry, the pollution of fresh waters was involved. (Jer. 9:11-15) Because they had forsaken his law, the Lord Almighty, the God of Israel, said, "See, I will make this people eat bitter food and drink poisoned water." (Jer. 9:15) NIV

In 1315, the people of Europe suffered from the worst floods in centuries. These disasters went beyond drowned persons and destroyed property. Crops in the field were ruined, and stored grain rotted. Topsoil was washed away. The aftermath of the floods lasted many years including famine and death. When the bubonic plague from Asia began spreading across Europe thirty-two years later, many of the people were convinced that God was punishing them for their sins.[86] **The third bowl of wrath is calamities involving rivers and springs of water.**

---

[85] Addison-Wesley, *World History Traditions and New Directions*, p. 375
[86] Addison-Wesley, *World History Traditions and New Directions*, p. 240

Then John heard *the angel in charge of the waters* say, *"You are righteous, O Lord, the One who is and who was and who is to be, because You have judged these things."* **16:5** ᴺᴷᴶⱽ Angels are assigned to be over special areas of God's creation. Four angels are in charge of the "**winds** of the earth" in 7:1. Another angel has "power over **fire**" in 14:18. And now we hear from "the angel in charge of the **waters**." Almighty God is working providentially in nature. The eternal Holy One proves that he is righteous by his use of natural calamities to judge the wicked that reject him and refuse to acknowledge him in their lives.

"For they have shed the blood of saints and prophets, and you have given them blood to drink." **16:6** Under the sixth seal God answered the cry of the saints that had been slain under the fifth seal. They had asked that their blood be avenged on those that dwell on the earth. (6:10-16) John heard one of the slain saints from the altar, saying, *"Even so, Lord God Almighty, true and righteous are your judgments."* **16:7** God avenges the sufferings of his servants. "Dearly beloved, avenge not yourselves, but rather give place unto wrath; for it is written, 'Vengeance is mine; I will repay,' says the Lord." (Romans 12:19)

And the fourth angel poured out his bowl upon the sun, and power was given to him to scorch men with fire. And men were scorched with great heat. **16:8-9** Jeremiah describes God's bowl of wrath upon the nobles of Judah when Jerusalem was destroyed in 586 BC. According to Lamentations 4:7-8, their once fair skin had become black, dry, and shriveled like unburied bodies under the desert sun.[87] The *sun* was involved also in the warning of the fourth trumpet (8:12).

---

[87] Ross Price, *The Wycliffe Bible Commentary*, p. 70

We may be able to see a twentieth century example of the fourth bowl of wrath in the death of James A. Pike. He was Bishop of the Episcopal Diocese of California from 1958 to 1966. Pike was one of the most publicized religious leaders in the country. His picture was featured on the cover of TIME magazine. His books were best sellers, including *If This Be Heresy*. He rejected the virgin birth of Jesus, the incarnation, the Trinity, and the infallibility of the Scriptures. In his last sermon, he said that an all-powerful, all-good, all-knowing God has never existed. His ungodly influence continues to this day due to his promotion of "the new morality." David W. Virtue wrote that his death in a Middle East desert was "a spiritual metaphor of his life." In the summer of 1969, Pike went to Israel to research Christian origins and to debunk the New Testament's account of the life of Jesus. Without a guide, he drove from Bethlehem on a desert road that he thought was leading to the Dead Sea, but the road came to a dead end. He was lost. He tried to turn his vehicle around, but got stuck in the sand. Several days later his body was found dead from exposure. The searing heat of the desert sun struck him. **The fourth bowl of wrath is the great heat of the sun.**

And they blasphemed the name of God who has power over these plagues; and they repented not to give him glory. **16:9** God has power over these calamities in nature. The first six bowls are poured out when men have the opportunity to repent. Those who survived these judgments of God were like those who heard the trumpets blowing, but did not repent. (Rev. 9:20-21)

And the fifth angel poured out his bowl upon the throne of the beast, and his kingdom was full of darkness; and they gnawed their tongues because of pain. **16:10** The beast is the symbol for ungodly rulers that persecute God's people. (13:1-2) The fifth bowl is the death of this kind of ruler and the great pain suffered by his loyal followers. The Roman Emperor Domitian was assassinated on September 18, AD 96.[88] Those who had worshiped him were overcome by great despair, while others rejoiced. It was like being plunged into total darkness. The ninth plague upon the Egyptians was total darkness. (Exodus 10:21-29) Their pain was emotional and mental as well as physical. The fifth trumpet is the suffering that comes as a consequence of sin. (Rev. 9:1-11) **The fifth bowl of wrath is the removal of an ungodly ruler.**

The followers of the beast *blasphemed the God of heaven because of their pains and their sores, and repented not of their deeds.* **16:11** They are suffering because of their sins, but instead of repenting, they blame God. With malicious words, they irreverently revile the true God of heaven.

And the sixth angel poured out his bowl upon the great river Euphrates; and the water thereof was dried up, that the way of the kings of the east might be prepared. **16:12** At the sounding of the sixth trumpet, four angels of war were released that had been bound at the great river Euphrates. (9:13-16) When the sixth bowl is poured out, the water of the great river Euphrates was dried up to prepare the way of the kings of the east. This is a reference to the fall of the Babylonian Empire in 539 BC. It was destroyed by the united kingdom of the Medes and the Persians. Darius the Mede and Cyrus the Persian were the conquering kings from the east of Babylon. The Euphrates ran through the center of the city of Babylon. Cyrus diverted the water of the river into a vast lake which had been constructed north of the city to carry off excess waters in the time of floods. By so doing, he dried up the river channel, and his armies were able to enter the city under the walls from the north

---

[88] Guy Edward F. Chilver, *Encyclopaedia Britannica*, Domitian

and the south.[89] The Greek historians Herodotus and Xenophon tell us that Babylon fell in this way. Over 150 years before the fall of Babylon, God's prophet Isaiah had predicted that the Medes and Persians (Elam) would defeat Babylon by drying up their rivers. It would be a surprise attack during a night of feasting.[90]

The sixth trumpet uses wars to warn sinners. The Roman Empire was being warned by invading armies from time to time. We have seen the parallelism between the trumpets and the seven bowls of wrath. Just as Babylon fell, the great Roman Empire would fall. Rome would be punished for its immoralities, idolatries, and persecutions against Christians. **The sixth bowl of wrath is wars between nations.**

And I saw three unclean spirits like frogs come out of the mouth of the dragon, and out of the mouth of the beast, and out of the mouth of the false prophet. **16:13** The three *unclean spirits* that John saw are compared to the plague of frogs upon Egypt. (Ex. 8:1-6) They were coming from three sources: from *the dragon*, who is Satan (12:9), from *the beast*, who symbolizes persecuting rulers (13:1-2), and from *the false prophet,* who represents false religions—the beast from the earth (13:11). *They are spirits of demons, working miracles, which go forth to the kings of the whole world, to gather them to the battle of that great day of God Almighty.* **16:14** The deceptive words of Satan, the propaganda of wicked governments, and the doctrines of false religions and philosophies are the spirits of demons that cause nations to go to battle against each other. *"The great day of God Almighty"* cannot be the final Day of the Lord, because the sixth bowl is being poured out. God's wrath will be complete in the seventh plague, when the seventh bowl is

---

[89] Albert E. Barnes, *Barnes Notes*, Isaiah 44:27
[90] Isaiah 21:2-9, Daniel 5, Isaiah 44:26-45:7

poured out. (15:1) Under the sixth seal, *"the great day of his wrath"* describes God's removal of sinful rulers and nations from power. (6:17) Throughout history, God has judged and punished wicked nations by allowing them to be defeated by other wicked nations in wars.

"Behold, I come as a thief. Blessed is he that watches and keeps his garments, lest he walk naked, and they see his shame." **16:15** Jesus interrupted the description of the sixth bowl of wrath to encourage each Christian to remain faithful. When he would come with invading armies to destroy the Roman Empire, the wicked unbelievers would be surprised as by *a thief* in the night. But the faithful Christian would know this bowl of wrath was coming; he would expect it and be prepared. Jesus had warned the church at Sardis that he was coming *as a thief*, because only a few of them had not defiled their garments with sinful living. (3:1-5) The unfaithful Christian would be exposed and would suffer shame. Also, encouragement was given to God's faithful servants when the sixth seal was opened. "For the great day of his wrath is come, and who shall be able to stand?" (6:17) The visions of the 144,000 and of the great multitude before God's throne reassured the saints that they would be able to stand. The bowls of wrath are poured out upon sinners. Christians have the victory!

And he gathered them together into a place called in the Hebrew tongue, Armageddon. **16:16** The widely accepted view is that Armageddon is the conclusive battle between the forces of good and evil. However, this popular view does not fit the context of Revelation 16:16. The *"them"* who are gathered together for the battle of Armageddon are *"the kings of the earth"* in verse 14. This battle is not between the forces of good and evil, but between the kings of the earth. The spirits of demons gathered these kings *"to the battle of the great day of God Almighty."* Wars between nations begin, when God in his sovereign providence has his angel to pour out the sixth bowl of wrath.

This battle should not be confused with the spiritual wars that the dragon and the beast make with Christ and his church, which describe persecutions endured by Christians.[91] As already observed, the church is not being considered in the first six bowls of wrath. These are God's judgments upon impenitent sinners.

The word ***Armageddon*** means Mount of Megiddo and is used to describe a famous battlefield on the Plain of Jezreel between the city of Megiddo and Mount Carmel in Israel. The good king was not always the victor at Armageddon. Josiah, the righteous king of Judah, was killed in a battle against Pharaoh Necho of Egypt at Megiddo.[92] God had promised that he would not destroy Jerusalem while Josiah was alive because he had humbled himself before the Lord.[93] With the death of Josiah, God began executing his plan to use the Babylonians (the Chaldeans) to punish the sinful nation of Judah.[94]

Armageddon is used symbolically to refer to any great decisive conflict. It is also called ***the battle of the great day of God Almighty*** in verse 14. The prophets simply described it as ***the day of the Lord***. It has come many times in history when God used wicked nations to punish other wicked nations. It was "the day of the Lord" or ***Armageddon*** when Assyria destroyed the city of Samaria and the kingdom of Israel in 721 BC. (Amos 5:18-27) Zephaniah is known as "The Day of the Lord Prophet" because he uses "the day of the Lord" to describe the destruction of Jerusalem by the Babylonians in 586 BC

---

[91] Revelation 11:7, 12:17, 13:7, 17:14, 19:19, 20:7-9
[92] 2 Kings 23:23-30
[93] 2 Kings 22:16-20
[94] Habakkuk 1:2-12

and the destruction of Assyria and its capital city of Nineveh in 612 BC. When Jeremiah predicted that Pharaoh Necho's Egyptian army would be defeated by Nebuchadnezzar king of Babylon, he said, "this is the day of the Lord of hosts." (Jeremiah 46:1-10) When Isaiah foretold that the Medes and Persians would overthrow the great Babylonian Empire, he called it "the day of the Lord." (Isa. 13:6-19, Isa. 21:2-9) In all these examples, the battle is never between good and evil. Wars between nations are the means by which they are judged and punished by God, "who rules in the kingdom of men." (Daniel 4:31-32) **Any great war between nations is the Battle of Armageddon.**

And the seventh angel poured out his bowl into the air, and there came a great voice out of the temple of heaven, from the throne, saying, "It is done." **16:17** Satan is "the prince of the power of the **air**." (Eph. 2:2) The seventh bowl of God's wrath was poured out upon the power of Satan, who is the source of all rebellion against God. No longer would Satan be able to exercise his evil influence upon the kingdoms of the earth. When the seventh trumpet sounded, loud voices in heaven proclaimed, "The kingdom of the world has become the kingdom of our Lord and of his Christ, and he shall reign forever and ever." (11:15) ᴱˢⱽ When *the seventh bowl* was poured out, a loud voice in heaven proclaimed, *"It is done."* God's wrath is completed. (15:1, 8) With the sounding of the seventh trumpet, God's final day of wrath had come and the dead were judged. (11:18) The temple in heaven was opened after the seventh trumpet sounded and after the seventh bowl of wrath was poured out. (Rev. 11:19; Rev. 15:8) The seventh trumpet and the seventh bowl describe the same events.

And there were flashes of lightning, rumblings, peals of thunder and a great earthquake such as there had never been since man was on the earth, so great was that earthquake. **16:18** ᴱˢⱽ The thunder and the lightning were revealing God's power and judgment. Catastrophes were occurring that men had never seen before. The destruction of the earth was beginning.

And the great city was divided into three parts, and the cities of the nations fell. And great Babylon came in remembrance before God, to give unto her the cup of the wine of the fierceness of his wrath. **16:19** Great Babylon represents the wicked worldly society. Rome was Babylon in the first century. (17:18) However, Babylon is not limited to the city of Rome, because *"the cities of the nations fell"* when "the great city was divided into three parts." Rome is only one of many cities of the world symbolized by Babylon. In the fourth view, Babylon is briefly mentioned for the first time. The fall of great Babylon is at the time of God's final judgment upon the wicked. (14:7-8) Those who have the mark of the beast will "drink of the wine of the wrath of God, which is poured out without mixture into the cup of his indignation." (14:9-10) At the conclusion of this fifth view, great Babylon is given "the cup of the wine of the fierceness of his wrath." (16:19) In the sixth view, an angel from heaven announces, "Babylon the great is fallen, is fallen." (18:2) The parallelism in Revelation is seen again.

And every island fled away, and the mountains were not found. **16:20** When the sixth seal was opened, "every mountain and island *were moved* out of their places." (6:14) Mountains and islands being moved describes the removal of governments and rulers from power from time to time in history. When the seventh bowl is poured out, "every island *fled away*, and the mountains *were not found*." They were not simply moved; they were removed and were seen no more. This is the final Day of the Lord that is described in 2 Peter 3:10-12. "But the day of the Lord will come as a thief in the night, in which the heavens shall pass away with a great noise, and the elements shall melt with fervent heat; the earth also and the works that are therein shall be burned up. Seeing then that all these things shall be dissolved, what manner of persons ought you to be in all holy conversation and godliness, looking for and hastening unto the coming of the day of God, wherein the heavens being on fire shall be dissolved, and the elements shall melt with fervent heat?" **This is the end of time.**

And there fell upon men a great hail out of heaven, every stone about the weight of a talent; and men blasphemed God because of the plague of the hail, for the plague thereof was exceeding great. **16:21** This is no ordinary judgment. Each hailstone weighed about a hundred pounds![95] In the same way, the description of the seventh trumpet concludes, "There were flashes of lightning, rumblings, peals of thunder, an earthquake *and heavy hail.*" (11:19) ᴱˢⱽ Because God's wrath had come, "the nations were angry." (11:18) And here, under the seventh bowl of wrath, *men blasphemed God.* (16:21) Instead of acknowledging their sins, they blamed God for their punishment. Jesus said, "There shall be wailing and gnashing of teeth." (Matthew 13:41-42) God's wrath is completed in the seventh bowl! (15:1) **The seventh bowl is the final judgment.**

---

[95] F. N. Peloubet, *Peloubet's Bible Dictionary*, p. 732, "Weights…"

Revelation 15-16 | **141**

Review Questions on Lesson 9

1. In this fifth view, seven _____ of _____ are being poured out to punish sinners.

2. Give an example of a calamity being a bowl of wrath to some and a trumpet of warning to others. _____
_____

3. In the seven last plagues (bowls of wrath), God's wrath is _____. 15:1

4. Those standing by what appeared to be a sea of glass were those who have the _____ over the beast.

5. A sea of glass is before the _____ of God. 4:6

6. The *fire* in the sea represents God's _____ of the wicked.

7. The victors were singing the song of _____ and the song of the _____.

8. The *harps* symbolize _____.

9. Who gave the seven angels the seven bowls of wrath?
_____

10. The temple was filled with _____ symbolizing God's wrath.

11. No one could enter the temple in heaven until the seven plagues were _____. (cf. 11:15-19)

12. The first bowl of wrath was poured out on the _____. God uses _____ to execute His wrath upon sinners. Compare with the first trumpet in Revelation 8:7

13. The second bowl of wrath is calamities at _____. Compare with second trumpet in Revelation 8:8.

14. The third bowl of wrath involves _____ and springs of _____. Compare with the third trumpet.

15. The fourth bowl was poured out on the _____, and sinful men were punished with great _____.

16. The fifth bowl was poured out on the _____ of the beast, like when _____ was assassinated.

17. The sixth bowl was poured out upon the great river, the River _____, and its water was _____, so that the way of the kings from the _____ might be prepared. Compare with the sixth trumpet in 9:13-16.
   This is a reference to what Old Testament event?
   _____
   _____

18. With the sixth bowl, God uses _____ to punish sinners.

19. Three unclean spirits were coming out of the mouth of the _____, the _____, and the false _____.

20. The three unclean spirits gather the kings of the earth to the battle of that great _____ of God Almighty.

21. "Armageddon" occurs when the _____ bowl is poured out, and it cannot be the final Day of the Lord, because God's wrath will be completed when the ____ bowl is poured out. (cf. 16:12-16 with 15:1 and 16:17-20.)

22. Armageddon symbolizes God's use of a _____ nation to punish another _____ nation, and the prophets called it "The _____ of the Lord."

23. The seventh angel poured out his bowl into the _____, the domain of _____, and a loud voice from heaven declared the final victory of good over evil by saying, "It is _____." And great _____ was remembered before God to receive his wrath, and the _____ were not found.

View 6

The Marriage of the Lamb

Revelation 17 – 19

NOTES

Babylon & the Beast
Revelation 17

The sixth view ends with the marriage of the Lamb, who is the victor. But first we'll see the worldly society and its destruction symbolized by the ancient city of Babylon.

Babylon was one of the oldest cities of the world. Soon after the flood, the people came to a plain in the land of Shinar, and they settled there. They built a city using brick for stone and asphalt for mortar. As an act of pride, they also began building a tower to make for them "a name". (Genesis 11:1-4) Rebellion was involved in building the tower. They were willfully refusing to obey God's command to scatter and fill the earth. (Genesis 9:1) The Lord caused the construction to cease when he confused their language in order to scatter them abroad over the earth. Therefore, the name of their city was called *"Babel"*. (Genesis 11:7-9) This Hebrew name for the city means *to confuse or to confound*. The Greeks called the city **Babylon**. The beginning of Babylon goes back to the tower of Babel.

Noah's great-grandson, Nimrod, organized a kingdom in the land of Shinar with the city of Babel in the center. (Genesis 10:1-10) This is the first time the word *kingdom* appears in the Bible.

In time, invading Sumerians replaced Nimrod's small kingdom, and their achievements were impressive. The Sumerians developed a system of writing known as *cuneiform*. Dikes, dams, and canals were constructed to irrigate fields. To improve their farming, they invented the plow. They studied the heavens and discovered seasonal equinoxes. Their observation of the different phases of the moon led to the development of a 12-month calendar. They had a system of mathematics based on the number 60. They divided the circle into 360 degrees. From the Sumerians, we have an hour divided into 60 minutes, and a minute into 60 seconds. The Sumerians also are credited for the invention of the potter's wheel and the discovery of how to make bronze by combining copper and tin. These achievements were passed on to the whole world.

Nebuchadnezzar made Babylon the most magnificent city in the ancient world. This Chaldean king began his reign in 605 BC and ruled for forty-three years over the new Babylonian Empire. He spared no expense in making Babylon a great city.

The fortifications of Babylon were impressive. Its walls were over 300 feet high and over 80 feet wide. There were many other protective walls within the city, including those that were on both sides of the river Euphrates, which ran through the middle of Babylon. Around the city was a wide and deep moat full of water.

Babylon was the most beautiful city of the world. Colorful enameled brick with pictures depicting life-sized lions, bulls, and dragons along with flowers and geometrical figures decorated its walls and palaces. The city gates and palace doors were made of cedar overlaid with bronze. The streets were laid out in a grid pattern like modern cities. A wide procession street extended from the main Ishtar gate through the middle of the city. Houses were of three and four stories with beautiful gardens. Babylon glittered with gold, silver, and precious jewels in its temples and palaces.

According to the Greeks, the Hanging Gardens of Babylon were one of the Seven Wonders of the World. This ancient marvel was built on a square base that was

400 feet on each side and rose in terraces creating an artificial mountain that was covered with rare flowers and many varieties of plants and trees.

The glory and spirit of ancient Babylon are summed up in these proud words of Nebuchadnezzar: "Is not this great Babylon, which I have built for the house of the kingdom by the might of my power and for the honor of my majesty?" (Daniel 4:30)

Babylon serves as the perfect symbol for the proud, worldly society of man. Babylon is "the world" in 1 John 2:16, "For all that is in the world, the lust of the flesh, the lust of the eyes, and the pride of life, is not of the Father, but is of the world." Babylon is personified as an attractive harlot in Revelation 17.

Then one of the seven angels who had the seven bowls came and talked with me, saying to me, "Come, I will show you the judgment of the great harlot who sits on many waters, with whom the kings of the earth committed fornication, and the inhabitants of the earth were made drunk with the wine of her fornication." **17:1-2** NKJV One of the angels of wrath will describe Babylon and her fall. This is fitting since the great city had been judged under the seventh bowl of wrath. (16:19)

Babylon is described as a prostitute, because the people of the world love her instead of God. She sits on many waters, which are the peoples, multitudes, nations, and languages of the world. (17:1, 15) Nebuchadnezzar loved and worshiped the work of his own hands. He gave the honor and praise that belong to God to the harlot Babylon. Other kings before and after Nebuchadnezzar have been guilty of spiritual fornication with the great cities of the world. Most men are "lovers of pleasures more than lovers of God." (2 Tim. 3:4) At the time of the writing of Revelation, Rome was Babylon, "that great city, which reigns over the kings of the earth." (17:18) The prostitute Babylon represents everything in the world that tempts, seduces, and draws people away from God. John was saying, "Do not love Babylon," when he wrote, "Love not the world, neither the things that are in the world. If man loves the world, the love of the Father is not in him." (1 John 2:15)

So he carried me away in the spirit into the wilderness. And I saw a woman sit upon a scarlet colored beast, full of names of blasphemy, having seven heads and ten horns. **17:3** This is the beast that rose up out of the sea in 13:1 and also came up out of the bottomless pit to kill God's two witnesses in 11:3-7. Ungodly governments support the glamorous cities of the world. Rome's glory was due to the Roman Empire. The scarlet color of the beast indicates the luxury and wealth that the empire brought to Rome.

The woman was arrayed in purple and scarlet, and adorned with gold and precious stones and pearls, having in her hand a golden cup full of abominations and the filthiness of her fornication. And on her forehead a name was written:

MYSTERY,
BABYLON THE GREAT,
THE MOTHER OF HARLOTS
AND OF THE ABOMINATIONS OF THE EARTH.

I saw the woman, drunk with the blood of the saints and with the blood of the martyrs of Jesus. And when I saw her, I marveled with great amazement. **17:4-6** NKJV The woman is representing "Babylon the Great, the mother of harlots." She attracts attention with her flashy clothing of purple and scarlet and with her ornaments of gold and precious stones and pearls. Even John marveled with great amazement when he saw her. Keep in mind that the harlot is personifying Babylon and other great cities of the world. When we reviewed the history of Babylon at the beginning of this chapter, were you not impressed with the great achievements and the glory of ancient Babylon? When you look at the great cities in the world, are you not amazed with the accomplishments of men? In the first century, men marveled at the greatness of Rome, and were excited with what she had to offer them.

The **golden cup** in the harlot's hand is beautiful on the outside, but is full of detestable and unclean things on the inside. Sin outwardly appears alluring and inviting, but its end is misery, disgusting filthiness, and death. Today, glittering cities invite us to engage in sinful pleasures and in dishonest gain. Also, in the great cities there are so many otherwise good activities that may so occupy our time that we are drawn away from God. The golden cup of Babylon represents everything that tempts us to sin and to forget God.

Babylon was **drunken with the blood of the saints** that were killed in Old Testament times **and with the blood of the martyrs of Jesus** (Christians). This is not repetition, but proof that Babylon is not limited to Rome. The Roman emperors were not alone in the persecution of Christians. The population of Rome demanded blood to be shed for their entertainment.

The angel asked John, **"Why did you marvel? I will tell you the mystery of the woman and of the beast that carries her, which has the seven heads and the ten horns." 17:7** NKJV The angel reveals the symbolism.

"The beast that you saw was, and is not, and shall ascend out of the bottomless pit and go into perdition." 17:8 The beast appears in history from time to time. He was seen in the time of the Egyptians, the Assyrians, the

Babylonians, the Medes and Persians, the Greeks, and the Romans. The beast imitates Christ with his resurrection. He was, and then he is not. But later he is seen again as he comes up out of the bottomless pit to persecute God's people again. The persecution does not last long, because the beast goes into perdition or destruction. First century readers of Revelation had seen the beast in Nero, who killed himself. Now, they were seeing the beast again in Domitian, who would be assassinated. The cycle of being alive, then dead, and resurrected continues until, at last, the beast is "cast alive into the lake of fire." (Rev. 19:20)

"And they that dwell on the earth shall wonder, whose names were not written in the Book of Life from the foundation of the world, when they behold the beast that was, and is not, and yet is." 17:8 From the earliest times, the unsaved masses of the world have marveled at the power of the beast. The beast seems indestructible. A persecutor may die, but another one arises. Satan through the beast is imitating Christ. The beast was, then he is not, and yet he is alive again. Christ said, ***"I am he who lives, and was dead, and behold, I am alive."*** (1:18) When Christ is alive, the beast is dead. When Christ is dead, the beast is alive. When Christ is alive again, the beast is dead again. Satan has his own resurrections, just like Christ. (Rev. 20:1-9) This again proves the repeating cycle of a long period of evangelism enjoyed by Christ and his church, followed by a short period of severe persecution suffered by Christians, and then victory when the church is able to preach again. This is the key to our understanding Revelation.

"Here is the mind which has wisdom. The seven heads are seven mountains on which the woman sits." 17:9 Ancient Rome was built literally on seven hills or mountains. ***"And there are seven kings." 17:10*** A mountain is a symbol for a kingdom, so the seven heads represent seven kings or kingdoms. (Jeremiah 51:1, 25,

Daniel 2:34-35, 44) Figuratively, the city of Rome was not only resting upon the Roman Empire but also upon the kingdoms that had preceded it. Besides having seven heads and ten horns, the beast in Revelation is like a lion, a bear, and a leopard. (13:1-2) Daniel had predicted that the Babylonian kingdom of Nebuchadnezzar would be replaced by three kingdoms: the Medo-Persian kingdom, the Greek kingdom, and the Roman kingdom. (Daniel 2) These four kingdoms are symbolized by "four great beasts" that came up from the sea in Daniel 7:3-7. The first was like a *lion,* and it represented Babylon. The second was like a *bear* representing the Medes and Persians. The third was like a *leopard* symbolizing the Greeks. The fourth beast had **ten horns**, and "the fourth beast shall be **the fourth kingdom** upon the earth." (Daniel 7: 23) The Roman Empire was the kingdom that replaced the Greeks. Before Daniel's time, the Egyptian kingdom and the Assyrian kingdom also had the characteristics of the beast.

"Five are fallen, and one is, and the other has not yet come." **17:10** At the time of the writing of Revelation, it could be said that the Roman Empire is the kingdom that *is*. Five kingdoms had already fallen. All of them had blasphemed God and persecuted his people. And for these sins, God had punished them. What were they?

The beast appeared first in a Pharaoh king of Egypt. He made slaves of God's people and blasphemed God by saying, "Who is the Lord that I should obey his voice?" (Exodus 5:2) God destroyed the Egyptian army in the Red Sea. Later, the Lord used the Babylonians to destroy the power of Egypt. (Jer. 46) The Egyptian kingdom was the first fallen kingdom.

The Assyrian Empire was the second kingdom to fall. With great cruelty, the Assyrians destroyed the city of

Samaria in taking captive the northern kingdom of Israel. They also invaded the southern kingdom of Judah. As the Assyrian army besieged Jerusalem, their king Sennacherib sent this blasphemous message to Hezekiah king of Judah: "Let not your God in whom you trust deceive you, saying, 'Jerusalem shall not be delivered into the hand of the king of Assyria.' Behold, you have heard what the kings of Assyria have done to all lands by destroying them utterly; and shall you be delivered?" (2 Kings 19:10-11) The angel of the Lord answered this proud king by killing 185,000 of the Assyrians in their camp at night. Sennacherib departed from Jerusalem and returned to his home in Nineveh, where he was killed by two of his own sons. (2 Kings 19:35-37) The prophecy of Nahum tells of the destruction of Nineveh and the fall of the great Assyrian empire.

The third fallen kingdom was the Babylonian Empire of Nebuchadnezzar. When he threatened the three young Jews who would not worship his golden image, he arrogantly asked, "And who is that God that shall deliver you out of my hands?" (Daniel 3:15) God showed his great power by miraculously saving Shadrach, Meshach, and Abed-Nego and by humbling this great king until he knew "that the most High rules in the kingdom of men, and gives it to whomsoever he will." (Daniel 3:19-30, Daniel 4:32) The night king Belshazzar saw the hand writing on the wall, Babylon fell to the Medes and Persians. (Daniel 5)

The Medes and Persians formed the fourth great kingdom. As a whole they treated the Jews well and allowed them to return to their homeland. However, Daniel was thrown into a den of lions, and the Jews were almost annihilated by official acts of the Medes and Persians. (Daniel 6; Esther) These terrible deeds were due to their desire to be worshiped as gods. This kingdom fell to the Greeks in 331 BC.

Alexander the Great and the Greek kings that followed him demanded to be worshiped as gods. Antiochus IV, the eighth king of the Seleucid dynasty, tried to force the Jews to adopt the Greek culture. He thought he was the incarnation of Jupiter and called himself *Theos Epiphanes*, meaning "God Illustrious"[96] or "God Manifest."[97] He made the Lord's temple in Jerusalem a shrine to Jupiter in 168 BC, and he further desecrated the temple by offering pigs on the altar. In his attempt to destroy the Holy Scriptures and all who were faithful to the Lord, he killed over a hundred thousand Jews. He himself died a very painful and humiliating death by the hand of God. (Daniel 8:25; 2 Maccabees 9:5-28)[98] The Greeks were the last to fall before the Roman Empire.

God's demonstration of his power over these five kingdoms that had fallen would have encouraged the first readers of Revelation to remain faithful regardless of the opposition. Those early Christians who were suffering persecution by the Roman Empire would have welcomed this message. The victory belongs to God and his people!

The other has not yet come. And when he comes, he must continue a short time. **17:10** The seventh head is any ruler or government after the Romans that will persecute the church. Seven symbolizes all remaining persecutors. The time of persecution is always for a relatively short time. If we should ever have to face severe persecution, let us be faithful unto death like those early Christians. (Rev. 2:10) The suffering is for a little while. The victory is with Christ!

---

[96] *McClintock-Strong Cyclopedia of Biblical...*, Antiochus IV, p. 272
[97] *Encyclopaedia Britannica*, "Antiochus IV"
[98] Second Maccabees is an uninspired book of the Apocrypha; however it relates the history between the Old and New Testaments.

***The beast that was, and is not, even he is the eighth, and is of the seven, and goes into perdition.* 17:11** The beast is the eighth kingdom. His kingdom is greater than any one of the kingdoms represented by the seven heads. The beast is more than the Roman Empire. He is all of the seven kingdoms combined. He has the swiftness of the leopard like Alexander the Great. He is powerful like the bear that represented the Medes and Persians. His seven heads have the royalty of the lion that symbolized Babylon, that proud city. He arrogantly blasphemes God and boasts of his own divine power. Whenever and wherever God's people are being persecuted, the beast is there.

The number *eight* symbolizes the power of God. Eight souls were saved in Noah's ark. (1 Peter 3:20) Abraham's covenant with the Lord required every male child to be circumcised on *the eighth day* to have God's blessing. (Genesis 17:7-14; Philippians 3:5) God's power was demonstrated when Jesus was raised from the dead on the first day of the week, and early Christians referred to this day as *the eighth day*.[99]

As already noted, the beast tries to imitate Christ. He has his own resurrection. He is also *the eighth*, and he claims to have divine power. Antiochus IV was *the eighth* ruler of the Seleucid dynasty, and he called himself "Illustrious God." Although Domitian was the eleventh Roman king, he was *the eighth* to establish his throne. Daniel's beast with ten horns was the Roman Empire. "And the ten horns out of this kingdom are ten kings that shall arise: and another shall rise after them." (Daniel 7:24) After the first ten Roman kings, there arose Domitian, whom Daniel described as a "little horn, before whom there were three of the first horns plucked up by

---

[99] Romans 1:3-4, Mark 16:9, *Epistle of Barnabas,* 15:9, an uninspired writing of the second century

the roots." (Dan. 7:8) Domitian's father was Vespasian, the ninth king, and his brother was Titus, the tenth. Before Vespasian came to the throne, the empire was unstable due to the assassinations of the three kings before him. Each one ruled for only a few months and was killed. Domitian, through his father, subdued these three kings and established a dynasty. The Roman historian Suetonius wrote that Domitian was arrogant and demanded that he be addressed as "Our Lord and Our God."[100] Domitian was part of the beast as he blasphemed God and persecuted Christians. When Christ returns, the beast **will go into perdition** which is described as "the lake of fire" in Revelation 19:20.[101]

And the ten horns which you saw are ten kings which have received no kingdom as yet; but receive power as kings one hour with the beast. **17:12** In Daniel's vision, ten horns belong to the fourth beast, the Roman Empire. (Daniel 7:23-24) Revelation's beast has ten horns on the head that *is*, the Roman Empire. Like Daniel's fourth beast, the ten horns represent ten kings, but they are not the same kings. Daniel's ten horns were the first ten kings of the Roman Empire, but of these ten kings only Nero is known for persecuting Christians. Revelation's ten kings rule the empire with the beast, and they all persecute the church— ***"These shall make war with the Lamb."*** (Rev. 17:14)

There were ten major persecutions against the church by the Roman Empire. They were brief, ***"only one hour with the beast,"*** in comparison to the time the church was free to preach openly. The first persecution lasted four years, AD 64 to 68, by Nero. The next 27 years brought peace to the church until the one-year tribulation by

---

[100] Suetonius, *Lives of the Twelve Caesars,* Domitian, Chapter 13, Section 2
[101] Read the comments on Revelation 1:9 for a response to those that interpret the seven heads of the beast to be seven Roman emperors.

Domitian from AD 95 to 96. During this short period of suffering, the book of Revelation was written. Eight more persecutions were coming against the church by ten more kings who had *"received no kingdom"* at that time. Two kings were to be involved in both the seventh and the tenth periods of persecution. The third persecution was by **Trajan**, the fourth by **Marcus Aurelius**, the fifth by **Severus**, the sixth by **Maximinus**, the seventh by **Decius and Gallus**, the eighth by **Valerian**, the ninth by **Aurelian**, and the tenth by **Diocletian** in the eastern half of the empire **and Maximian** in the western half. Christians were not constantly being mistreated by the Romans. During the 249 years from the beginning of Nero's persecution until it all ended in 313, Christians were without severe persecution 80 percent of the time – about 200 years! They had long periods of evangelism.

These have one mind, and shall give their power and strength to the beast. **17:13** All of these ten Roman emperors were united in their willingness to blaspheme God and persecute his people. They gave themselves and their authority as instruments of the ageless beast that fights against God and his saints.

These shall make war with the Lamb, and the Lamb shall overcome them, for he is Lord of lords and King of kings; and they that are with him are called, and chosen, and faithful. **17:14** This is the theme verse of Revelation. Christ the Lamb will conquer these ten Roman emperors, because he is the King of kings. Christians are God's chosen people that have been called out of darkness into his light. (1 Peter 2:9) They are to be faithful unto death. (Rev. 2:10) The church is victorious with Christ the King!

And the angel said to me, "The waters that you saw, where the prostitute is seated, are peoples and multitudes, nations, and languages." **17:15** ᴱˢⱽ We now are taken back to the harlot Babylon *who sits on many waters.* (17:1)   The great masses of people from various nations are both powerful and unstable as a flood of many waters. They support the great worldly society represented by the harlot Babylon. Rome was Babylon in the first century.

"And the ten horns which you saw on the beast, these will hate the harlot, make her desolate and naked, eat her flesh and burn her with fire." **17:16** ^{NKJV} These ten persecuting Roman emperors did not hate the ways of Rome. In fact, they loved her sinful ways. They hated the harlot in the sense that an indulgent father hates his child. "He that spares his rod *hates* his son." (Proverbs 13:24) The actions of these kings were responsible for the fall of Rome. "Righteousness exalts a nation, but sin is a reproach to any people." (Proverbs 14:34)

God has put it in their hearts to fulfill his will, and to agree, and to give their kingdom unto the beast, until the words of God shall be fulfilled. **17:17**   We are reminded that "the most High rules in the kingdom of men." (Daniel 4:17) At the time of the Exodus, the Lord said to Pharaoh, "Even for this same purpose have I raised you up, that I might show my power in you, and that my name might be declared throughout all the earth." (Romans 9:17) God does not make these rulers evil, but he gives them the opportunity to believe Satan's lies and give their power to the beast. (2 Thessalonians 2:9-12) The ten persecutions against the church served God's purposes. The church was purified through suffering (1 Peter 1:6-7), and the Lord proved that the great Roman Empire could "not prevail against it." (Matthew 16:18) God is in control.

And the woman which you saw is that great city which reigns over the kings of the earth. **17:18**   At the time Revelation was being written, Rome was that great city. Babylon was the great city that reigned over the kings of the earth during the time of Nebuchadnezzar. (Daniel 4:22, 28-30) But ancient Babylon is *"the mother of harlots and abominations of the earth."* (17:5) There have been and will be many harlots symbolized by Babylon. Babylon may be seen in other great cities of the world having an ungodly influence. Just as the beast is not limited to the Roman Empire, the symbol of Babylon is not limited to Rome.

Review Questions on Lesson 10

1. What does ancient Babylon symbolize?
   _____

2. Babylon is personified as a _____ in chapter 17.

3. What did one of the seven angels of God's wrath promise to show John? _____

4. What are "the many waters" on which the harlot sits?
   _____

5. Describe the beast upon which the woman sits. 17:3
   _____

6. The woman was arrayed in _____ and _____ and decked with _____ and precious _____ and _____, having a _____ cup in her hand.

7. What was written on the woman's forehead? 17:5
   _____
   _____

8. What does the golden cup represent? _____
   _____

9. The woman was drunk with the blood of the saints of the _____ _____ and the blood of the martyrs of _____.

10. Imitating Christ, the beast _____ and then he is _____, and he _____ out of the bottomless pit. 17:8

11. The seven heads of the beast are seven _____ on which the woman sits.

12. The seven heads also represent seven _____. 17:10

13. How many of these seven kings (or kingdoms) had fallen? _____

14. Name the five great persecuting kingdoms that had fallen.
    (1) _____
    (2) _____
    (3) _____
    (4) _____
    (5) _____

15. The _____ Empire was the "one" head that *"is."*

16. What does the seventh head of the beast represent?
    _____

17. The _____ is "the eighth" kingdom, and he represents all of the seven kingdoms combined.

18. What number symbolizes the power of God? _____

19. The ten horns of the beast belong to the head representing _____ Empire, and in Revelation they symbolize ten kings that would give their power to the _____. 17:12-13

20. These ten kings have power (authority) with the beast for how long? 17:12 _____ _____

21. These ten kings will *"make war"* with the _____, who is the _____ of lords, and _____ of kings.

22. The _____, _____, and _____ are with the victorious Lamb. 17:14

23. What in 17:18 proves that Babylon in the first century was Rome? _____

God Almighty Reigns
Revelation 18 – 19

And after these things, I saw another angel come down from heaven, having great power; and the earth was lightened with his glory. **18:1** An angel having one of the seven bowls of God's wrath has described the great harlot Babylon and the beast in the previous chapter. Then John saw another angel coming down from heaven in great power and bright glory to announce the fall of Babylon. This angel could be the archangel mentioned in 1 Thessalonians 4:16, "For the Lord himself will descend from heaven with a shout, with the voice of an archangel, and with the trump of God."

And he cried mightily with a strong voice, saying, "Babylon the great is fallen, is fallen, and is become the habitation of devils, and the hold of every foul spirit, and a cage of every unclean and hateful bird." **18:2** In 539 BC, the Medes and Persians conquered the city of Babylon as predicted by the prophets.[102] Other prophecies predicted that Babylon would be "inhabited no more forever," but would become the dwelling place for desert animals and birds.[103] The Medes and Persians did not destroy the city, but they made Babylon a second capital. Alexander the Great died in the city of Babylon in 323 BC. The city gradually decayed. Bricks were taken from this ancient city to repair canals and to build new cities. After the third century AD, Babylon became the deserted place predicted by the prophets.

Revelation's prophecies against Babylon were not completely fulfilled when the Roman Empire fell in AD 476. Like ancient Babylon, its fall was just the beginning of God's judgments. The city of Rome is a popular tourist attraction even today. The complete fall of Babylon, the mother of harlots, will include the fall of all the great cities of the world that allure men away from God.

---

[102] Isaiah 21:2-9; Daniel 5:28-31
[103] Jeremiah 50:35, 39; Isaiah 13:20-22

"For all the nations have drunk of the wine of the wrath of her fornication, the kings of the earth have committed fornication with her, and the merchants of the earth have become rich through the abundance of her luxury." **18:3** NKJV All nations will suffer God's wrath, because they have become intoxicated with the immoralities, the wealth, and the power of such worldly cities as ancient Babylon and Rome.

And John heard another voice from heaven saying, *"Come out of her, my people, that you be not partakers of her sins, and that you receive not of her plagues."* **18:4** This second voice is the voice of the Lord urging his people not to share in the sins of the wicked world, but to come out of spiritual Babylon. Those who want to be a part of the sinful city will receive her plagues. Paul wrote similar words to the Corinthians: "Be ye not unequally yoked together with unbelievers: for what fellowship has righteousness with unrighteousness?" He concluded, "Come out from among them and be ye separate, says the Lord, and touch not the unclean thing, and I will receive you." (2 Cor. 6:14, 17)

"For her sins have reached unto heaven, and God has remembered her iniquities. Reward her even as she rewarded you, and double unto her double according to her works: in the cup which she has filled, fill to her double." **18:5-6** The sins of Babylon were piled up higher than the tower of Babel, for they reached to heaven. "Everything is uncovered and laid bare before the eyes of him to whom we must give account." (Heb. 4:13) NIV God knows and remembers the sins of Babylon. According to the natural law of sowing and reaping, Babylon would reap not only **what** she had sown but also much **more** than she had sown. (Gal. 6:7-8, Hosea 8:7)

"In the measure that she glorified herself and lived luxuriously, in the same measure give her torment and sorrow; for she says in her heart, 'I sit as queen, and am no widow, and will not see sorrow.' Therefore her plagues will come in one day—death and mourning and famine. And she will be utterly burned with fire, for strong is the Lord God who judges her." **18:7-8** Both ancient Babylon and Rome were proud cities, and they said, "I sit as a queen...and will

not see sorrow." (Isaiah 47:7, 10) Even today, Rome proudly calls herself, "The Eternal City." This should be enough proof that Revelation 18 was not completely fulfilled in Rome's fall in AD 476. Rome is still glorifying herself. Babylon will be humbled and punished to the same degree that she has lived in pride and wealth. This punishment is yet to come, because the city of Rome has not been completely consumed with fire. *Her plagues will come in a single day*; and *she will be burned up with fire.* ESV That *"one day"* will be the last great "day of the Lord" when "the earth also and the works that are therein shall be burned up." (2 Peter 3:10-12)

"The kings of the earth who committed fornication and lived luxuriously with her will weep and lament for her, when they see the smoke of her burning, standing at a distance for fear of her torment, saying, 'Alas, alas, that great city Babylon, that mighty city! For in one hour your judgment has come.'" **18:9-10** NKJV The lament over the fall of Babylon by kings, merchants, and seamen is in **verses 9-19**. Their power, their luxuries, and their riches depended upon Babylon. When Rome fell in AD 476, the rulers that were allied with Rome lost their power; merchants and seamen lost their wealth. Their losses will be even greater on the last great day of the Lord, when Babylon, the worldly society of men, is completely burned up! "And the world is passing away, and the lust of it; but he who does the will of God abides forever." (1 John 2:17) NKJV

"Rejoice over her, O heaven, and you saints and apostles and prophets, because God has pronounced judgment for you against her." **18:20** NASB The Lord has promised, "Vengeance is mine, I will repay." (Romans 12:19) When Babylon falls at the end of time, all who have ever suffered because of the wicked world will be avenged. Babylon will be repaid. The fall of Babylon is mentioned in Revelation 14:8-16 for the first time along with the eternal punishment of the wicked. Babylon was remembered before God and given the cup of the wine of God's wrath when the seventh bowl was poured out at the end of time. (16:19) And here in the eighteenth chapter, we have read that Babylon the great is

fallen (v. 2), that God has remembered Babylon's iniquities (v. 5), and she is to be repaid double according to her works (v. 6). These views are parallel. God's ultimate vengeance upon Babylon is on that last great day of God's wrath and judgment. (Romans 2:5-11)

And a mighty angel took up a stone like a great millstone and cast it into the sea, saying, "Thus with violence shall that great city of Babylon be thrown down, and shall be found no more at all." 18:21 When the mighty angel threw the great stone into the sea, it was seen no more. This demonstration was given to illustrate the complete disappearance of Babylon. Rome can still be seen today, hundreds of years after its fall in AD 476. However, when Babylon falls, she will not be found "at all". The earth will be "dissolved" on the last great day of the Lord. (2 Peter 3:11) When something like sugar is dissolved in water, you do not see it anymore. The words *not...anymore* are repeated like an echo in the following verses.

The sound of harpists, musicians, flutists, and trumpeters shall not be heard in you anymore. No craftsman of any craft shall be found in you anymore, and the sound of a millstone shall not be heard in you anymore. The light of a lamp shall not shine in you anymore and the voice of bridegroom and bride shall not be heard in you anymore. 18:22-23 NKJV All of these things are still in Rome today. This is not a description of the fall of Rome in 476. Babylon will be destroyed completely and vanish from sight, because all nations were deceived by her sorcery *and in her was found the blood of prophets, and of saints, and of all that were slain upon the earth. 18:23-24*

After these things John heard a loud voice of a great multitude in heaven, saying, *"Hallelujah! Salvation and glory and power belong to our God!" 19:1* NIV After seeing the vision of the fall of Babylon, John hears a great multitude in heaven praising God. *Hallelujah* means "Praise the Lord." The heavenly chorus is saying, "Praise the Lord!" The only place that the word *Hallelujah* appears in the New Testament is in this chapter.

"True and righteous are His judgments, because He has judged the great harlot who corrupted the earth with her fornication; and He has avenged on her the blood of His servants shed by her." **19:2** ᴺᴷᴶⱽ The Judgment Day has come! The great harlot Babylon has been judged. God is being praised for his victory over the wicked world. This heavenly scene has been described previously in 7:9-17, in 11:15-19, and in 14:1-11. In each scene, God is worshiped and praised by a great multitude for the salvation of his servants and for his great glory, honor, and power.

And again they shouted: "Hallelujah! The smoke from her goes up for ever and ever!" The twenty-four elders and the four living creatures fell down and worshiped God, who was seated on the throne. And they cried: "Amen, Hallelujah!" **19:3-4** ᴺᴵⱽ The twenty-four elders represent the faithful leaders of both the old and the new covenants. This is further proof that the harlot is not limited to the city of Rome. God's servants in Old Testament times also had suffered because of the wicked world, and they now rejoice in her destruction. The elders and the four cherubim before God's throne are saying, "Let it be so! Praise the Lord!" The harlot Babylon is being punished for sins that go all the way back to the tower of Babel.

The Marriage of the Lamb

Then a voice came from the throne, saying: "Praise our God, all you his servants, you who fear him, both small and great!" **19:5** A great multitude was shouting, *"Hallelujah! For our Lord God Almighty reigns."* **19:6** ᴺᴵⱽ The sound of the great multitude was like the voice of the 144,000 that were with the victorious Lamb standing on Mount Zion in 14:1-3. The voice is announcing God's ultimate and complete victory over all powers that oppose him. "The kingdom of the world has become the kingdom of our Lord and of his Christ, and he shall reign forever and ever!" (11:15) ᴺᴵⱽ The end of the world has come. Christ has delivered "the kingdom to God the Father" after he has "put down all rule and all authority and power." (1 Cor. 15:24) The climax of Handel's "Hallelujah Chorus" is *"The Lord God Omnipotent reigns!"* (19:6) ᴷᴶⱽ

"Let us be glad and rejoice and give honor to him: for the marriage of the Lamb is come." 19:7 The marriage of Christ the Lamb to his bride, the church, takes place in heaven after the fall of Babylon, the Judgment Day. The Jewish marriage consisted of four steps.

The Betrothal, to be promised in marriage, was the first step. The Jewish betrothal was more binding than our engagement today. Before witnesses, terms of the marriage contract were accepted. Included in the terms was the **dowry**, which was paid to the parents of the bride. Then they prayed for God's blessing to be upon the marriage, and the two were legally husband and wife, although their marriage was not consummated at this time. (Matthew 1:18-20) The dowry that Jacob paid for Rachel was seven years of service to her father Laban. (Genesis 29:18-20) Jesus Christ gave his own blood for his bride, the church. (Acts 20:28, Ephesians 5:25) The terms of our marriage to Christ are set forth in the new covenant. If we desire to be part of the church, the bride of Christ, we must believe in Christ Jesus and confess him before men. (Rom. 10:10, Matt. 10:32) Forsaking all others and pledging our faithfulness to Christ, we must "repent, and be baptized…in the name of Jesus Christ for the remission of sins." (Acts 2:38) The church is now legally Christ's bride.

The Interval was the second step in a Jewish marriage. This was the period between the betrothal and marriage feast. During this time the groom made his house ready for his bride. Jesus said in John 14:2, "In my Father's house are many mansions … I go to prepare a place for you." Also, at this time, the bride prepared herself and her wedding dress. ***"And his wife has made herself ready. And to her was granted that she should be arrayed in fine linen, clean and white: for the fine linen is the righteousness of saints." 19:7-8*** Christ has helped his bride to get ready. He died for her "that He might sanctify and cleanse her with the washing of water by the word, that He might present her to Himself a glorious church, not having spot or wrinkle or any such thing, but that she might be holy and without blemish." (Eph. 5:25-27) NKJV The church is clothed with Christ, "for as many of you as have been baptized into Christ have put on Christ." (Galatians 3:27)

As the bride of Christ, we have been "created in Christ Jesus unto good works, which God has before ordained that we should walk in them." (Ephesians 2:10) Although it is "not by works of righteousness which we have done" that God saved us, we should "be careful to maintain good works." (Titus 3:5, 8) The wedding dress of Christ's bride is made of fine linen representing "the righteousness of the saints."

The Procession was the third step, and it came at the end of the interval. The groom, accompanied by his friends, went to the house of his bride and returned with her to his own house for the wedding. Jesus said, "I will come again and receive you unto myself; that where I am, there you may be also." (John 14:3) "The Son of man shall come in the glory of his Father with his angels." (Matthew 16:27) Christ is not coming to reign for a thousand years in the bride's house on earth. When he comes, he will take his bride to his Father's house in heaven, to the place he has prepared for her.

The Wedding Feast was the final step of the Jewish marriage. Jesus attended such a wedding feast in Cana of Galilee. (John 2:1) Then the angel said to John, ***"Write: 'Blessed are they which are called to the marriage supper of the Lamb!'"*** **19:9** The angel who is speaking is probably the one who began this section by describing the judgment of the harlot Babylon in Revelation 17:1. What a contrast between the pure bride of Christ and the harlot! As they face trials and temptations, Christians need to remember their glorious hope. What a blessing it is to be invited to the marriage supper of the Lamb! Jesus compared the kingdom of heaven to a marriage supper, and he concluded the parable by saying, "For many are called, but few are chosen." (Matthew 22:1-14) The invitation of the gospel is sent out to all, but only those who will come into Christ's church, his bride, and remain faithful will enjoy the marriage supper, which symbolizes the wonderful relationship that the church has with Christ in heaven. The angel adds, ***"These are the true sayings of God."*** **19:9** God's truth stands in contrast with the harlot's lies and false hopes. (18:7)

And I fell at his feet to worship him. But he said to me, "See that you do not do that! I am your fellow servant, and of your brethren who have the testimony of Jesus. Worship God!" **19:10** ᴺᴷᴶⱽ The awesome things that he was seeing and hearing so overpowered John that he fell down in reverence at the angel's feet. Immediately, the angel told him not to do it, because he is a fellow servant with John and his brethren in witnessing that Jesus is Lord. The angel instructed John to worship God. Referring to the birth of Christ, Hebrews 1:6 says, "When God brings his firstborn into the world, he says, 'Let all God's angels worship him.'" ᴺᴵⱽ Worship Christ!

"The testimony of Jesus is the spirit of prophecy." **19:10** The testimony that Jesus is the Christ is the fulfillment of prophecy. The Holy Spirit inspired both the prophecy and the testimony.[104] This transitional statement introduces the next vision of the Rider on the White Horse. John is taken back in time with a vision of Christ in his warfare against the kings of the earth that are symbolized by the beast. Christ, the Rider on the White Horse, is worthy to receive the love and adoration of his bride, the church.

Then John saw heaven opened. *And behold a white horse; and he that sat upon him was called Faithful and True.* **19:11** Christ is the Rider on the white horse who conquers with the gospel in 6:2. John now sees Christ as the conqueror who judges the beast upon which Babylon sat. Jesus describes himself as "the faithful and true witness" in Revelation 3:14. He has judged Babylon, and now he will judge the beast.

His eyes were as a flame of fire, and on his head were many crowns; and he had a name written that no man knew, but he himself. **19:12** The description of his eyes goes back to the first vision of the Son of Man in the midst of the seven lampstands. (1:12-14) With eyes of flaming fire, he sees all things and judges righteously. The crowns on his head are **diadems** of authority and power. He has all authority and power in heaven and on earth. (Matthew 28:18) The name

---

[104] 2 Peter 1:21, Matthew 16:15-17, John 15:26

that no one knows except Christ himself is probably referring to his unique redemptive work, because a name may denote the work of a person. (5:3-10) Only Christ knows what he went through to save us.

***And he was clothed with a vesture dipped in blood, and his name is called The Word of God.* 19:13** The blood on his garment may symbolize the blood he shed when crucified. Through his death, he defeated the devil. (Hebrews 2:14) Christ has redeemed us by his blood. (Rev. 5:5-13) The blood on his garment may also be that of his enemies, representing a great slaughter. (Isaiah 63:1-6, Rev. 14:20) Christ is *The Word of God*, who "was made flesh, and dwelt among us." (John 1:1, 14)

***And the armies in heaven, clothed in fine linen, white and clean, followed Him on white horses.* 19:14** NKJV Christ, the Rider on the white horse, has the support of heaven's armies, and they are all riding on white horses. The seven angels of God's wrath are "clothed in pure and white linen." (Rev. 15:6) Their bowls of wrath are similar to the hardships that are associated with the red, black, and pale horses in Revelation 6:3-8.

***And out of his mouth goes a sharp sword, that with it he should smite the nations: and he shall rule them with a rod of iron: and he treads the winepress of the fierceness and wrath of Almighty God.* 19:15** His weapon is the word of God, that is "sharper than any two-edged sword." (Heb. 4:12) In the first vision, the Son of Man had a sharp two-edged sword that went out of his mouth. (1:16) The war with the beast is a spiritual battle. Christ conquers his enemies with the gospel, which is a message both of salvation and of condemnation. "Go ye into all the world and preach the gospel to every creature. He that believes and is baptized shall be saved, but he that believes not shall be damned." (Mark 16:15-16) His scepter is a rod of iron, the instrument of punishment. The Christ shall break the nations "with a rod of iron." (Psalm 2:9) He will put an end to all rule and all authority and power of men (1 Corinthians 15:24), and he will say to the wicked, "Depart from me, you cursed, into the everlasting fire prepared for the devil and his angels." (Matthew 25:41) He will execute God's judgment and great wrath that is symbolized by a winepress, as in Revelation 14:19-20.

And he has on his vesture and on his thigh a name written: KING OF KINGS AND LORD OF LORDS. **19:16** Christ will conquer all those that make war with him, because he is the King of kings and the Lord of lords. (Rev. 17:14)

Then John saw *an angel standing in the sun; and he cried with a loud voice, saying to all the fowls that fly in the midst of heaven, "Come and gather yourselves together to the supper of the great God; that you may eat the flesh of kings, and the flesh of horses and of them that sit on them, and the flesh of all men, both free and bond, both small and great."* **19:17-18** This great slaughter of the wicked is a symbolic vision, not to be taken literally. So that he can be clearly seen and heard, the angel is standing in the sun that will bake the dead bodies. He is inviting the birds to come and feed on the flesh of the dead. This is the supper of God's wrath, and it should not be connected with the marriage supper of the Lamb in verse nine.

And John saw *the beast and the kings of the earth, and their armies, gathered together to make war against him that sat on the horse and against his army.* **19:19** This is a symbolic view of the history of the beast. The seven heads of the beast represent seven groups of persecutors against God's people, beginning with Pharaoh of Egypt. These are *the kings of the earth* who are with the beast. (Rev. 17:10) Christ, the Word of God, appeared in the burning bush as the Angel of the Lord to call upon Moses to deliver the nation of Israel from their bondage in Egypt. (Exodus 3:2, Hebrews 3:1-6) David wrote, "Why do the nations rage, and the people plot a vain thing? The kings of the earth set themselves, and the rulers take counsel together against the Lord and against His Anointed." (Psalm 2:1-2; Acts 4:19-31) ^{NKJV}

This war is not a literal battle at the end of time, but rather the constant struggle throughout history between the forces of good and evil that is seen in persecutions against God's people. The army of Christ on earth is composed of God's faithful servants who have been redeemed by the blood of the Lamb. (Rev. 12:10-11) His armies in heaven include the angels that sound the seven trumpets and pour out the seven bowls of God's wrath. The ultimate victory of Christ and his church is assured by his previous victories over the many persecutors of God's people.

And the beast was captured, and with him the false prophet, who worked signs in his presence, by which he deceived those who received the mark of the beast and those who worshiped his image. These two were cast alive into the lake of fire burning with brimstone. **19:20** NKJV The beast representing persecutors and the false prophet representing false religions are judged and are punished eternally in the lake of fire. Just as Babylon shall not be anymore, false religions and persecutors shall not be around anymore to harm God's servants.

And the rest were killed with the sword which proceeded from the mouth of Him who sat on the horse. And the birds were filled with their flesh. **19:21** NKJV The "rest" refers to the followers of the beast and of the false prophet. This figurative language describes the Judgment Day and the eternal punishment of the wicked. The word of God is described as a two-edged sword in Hebrews 4:12. Jesus said, "He that rejects me, and receives not my words, has one that judges him: the word that I have spoken, the same shall judge him in the last day." (John 12:48) "And anyone not found written in the Book of Life was cast into the lake of fire, (Rev. 20:15) which "is the second death." (Rev. 20:14)

We have come to the end of the sixth view, with the marriage of the Lamb and with his victory over the beast and the false prophet and their followers. The end of time has come once more.

NOTES

Revelation 18-19 | **173**

Review Questions on Lesson 11

1. The angel announcing Babylon's fall had great _____ and bright _____ that illuminated the earth.

2. Were all the prophecies against Babylon fulfilled when the city of Rome fell in AD 476? _____

3. "Come out of (Babylon), my people, that you be not partakers of her _____." 18:4

4. The sins of Babylon reached unto _____. 18:5

5. Babylon says in her heart that she is a _____ and will not see _____. 18:7

6. Even today, Rome calls herself "The _____ City."

7. Babylon's judgment will come upon her in one _____ and in one _____. 18:8, 10

8. Babylon "shall be utterly _____ with _____."

9. Who will weep over Babylon? 18:9, 11, 17-19 _____
   _____

10. Who will rejoice over the fall of Babylon? 18:20
    _____

11. How did "a mighty angel" show the violent and complete destruction of Babylon? 18:21 _____
    _____

12. Babylon "shall be _____ no more at all." 18:21

13. After the fall of Babylon, what was a loud voice in heaven saying? 19:1 _____
    _____

14. God's judgments are _____ and _____.

15. What was the great multitude saying in 19:6?
    _____

16. The _____ of the Lamb takes place after the great Day of Judgment. 19:7

17. The four steps of a Jewish marriage:
    (1) _____, (2) _____,
    (3) _____, (4) _____.
    How does each step relate to Christ and his church?

18. The Lamb's wife has made herself _____. 19:7

19. The Rider on the white horse called is called _____ and _____, and in righteousness he _____ and makes _____. 19:11

20. This Rider's eyes are like _____, and on his head were _____ _____.
    His garment was dipped in _____,
    and his name is called _____.

21. With what did the Rider on the white horse strike the nations? _____

22. Psalm 2:9 predicted that the Christ would rule "with a rod of _____."

23. What name was written on the Rider's robe and on his thigh? 19:16 _____

24. Who gathered "to make war" against the white horse's Rider and his army? _____

25. The beast and the false prophet were cast alive into the lake of _____. 19:20

26. Revelation 19:21 is describing the _____ Day and the eternal _____ of the wicked.

View 7

The Victorious Church

Revelation 20 – 22

NOTES

The Millennium & The Judgment

Revelation 20

The seventh view of the victorious church begins with chapter twenty. Satan is the last enemy of the church to be judged. Already, we have seen the judgment of four enemies: those who have the mark of the beast in chapter 14, the harlot Babylon in chapter 18, and the beast and the false prophet in chapter 19. In this last view, we shall see Satan being bound and released and finally being cast into the lake of fire in verse 10. The twentieth chapter concludes with the Judgment Day before the great white throne of God.

John saw an angel come down from heaven, having the key of the bottomless pit and a great chain in his hand. **20:1** This angel is one of God's heavenly messengers. He is not the fallen angel of the bottomless pit to whom the key "was given" in Revelation 9:1-11, because Satan cannot bind and cast out Satan. (Mark 3:23-27) *The key* and *the chain* are symbolic of the power to release and to restrain. Christ has the keys of death and Hades in Revelation 1:18. The angels that sinned are "reserved in everlasting chains under darkness unto the judgment of the great day." (Jude 6) This angel of God has the power to bind and release Satan.

And he laid hold on the dragon, that old serpent, which is the Devil and Satan, and bound him a thousand years and cast him into the bottomless pit and shut him up and set a seal on him, that he should deceive the nations no more till the thousand years should be fulfilled: and after that he must be loosed a little season. **20:2-3** God's angel took hold of Satan, who is identified as the dragon, the great persecutor of Christ and his church. (12:9) He is also that old serpent, who first brought sin and suffering into the world. (Genesis 3) The purpose of binding Satan is to keep him from persecuting the church. When Satan is released from the pit, he deceives the nations, and they make war against the saints. (20:3, 7-9)

The power of God to limit Satan is seen in the story of Job. At first God protected Job completely from Satan's power. (Job 1:10) Then God put all that Job had into Satan's hands. But he still restricted him, saying, "Do not lay a hand on his person." (Job 1:12) NKJV Later, God permitted Satan to afflict Job with painful boils, but he was not allowed to take his life. (Job 2:4-7)

As long as the beast is in the bottomless pit, he cannot persecute the church. But when the beast comes up out of the bottomless pit, he makes ***war*** against God's servants. (11:7, 13:8) The beast receives his power from the dragon, who is Satan. (13:2) Satan figuratively then is bound in the bottomless pit when God will not permit his people to be severely persecuted. God has set a ***seal*** on him. The seal shows God's authority to restrict Satan's power.

While Satan is bound in the bottomless pit, his power is being limited only in the area of persecution. He still has power in other areas such as hardships and temptations. Satan and his angels are "in everlasting chains" (Jude 6), yet "the devil, as a roaring lion, walks about seeking whom he may devour." (1 Peter 5:8) A dog may be chained to a stake, but he is dangerous to any person who enters the circle created by the radius of his chain. (For more information on the bottomless pit, see comments on Revelation 9:1.)

The first readers of Revelation 20 were Christians who were being persecuted by the Roman Emperor Domitian. John was in "the tribulation" (1:9) when he wrote the book. These first-century Christians would be encouraged when they read that Satan would be bound and cast into the bottomless pit, because this meant the end of Domitian's persecution. They also realized that when Satan was released, Christians would be persecuted again, but only *for a little season* or a little while. (20:3)

The words of Jesus in Revelation 1:18 reveal the key that unlocks the mystery of Revelation 20:1-10, along with the rest of the book. Jesus said, *"I am he who lives, and was dead, and behold, I am alive forevermore."*

During his earthly ministry of three-and-a-half years, Jesus was **alive**. During this time he was able to teach. The opposition and blasphemy that he encountered did not hinder his work, but provided an opportunity for him to demonstrate his great power and wisdom. Satan was being bound during this period. (Matthew 12:28-29)

Jesus was **dead** for three days following his crucifixion. He was not able to teach. Satan appeared to be victorious. He had killed Jesus by deceiving the rulers. (1 Cor. 2:8) The disciples of Jesus felt defeated. They had given up all hope. But Satan's apparent victory was only temporary.

When Jesus was raised from the dead, he was **alive** again forevermore. The ultimate victory belongs to Christ and his church. (1 Cor. 15:1-5, 55-58) Following his resurrection, Jesus sent fire and judgment on the day of Pentecost. In Luke 22:30, Jesus promised his apostles that they would "sit on thrones judging the twelve tribes of Israel." Divided tongues "as of fire" were on the heads of the apostles on the day of Pentecost, and Peter's sermon was one of judgment upon those who by lawless hands had crucified Jesus. (Acts 2:23) When he returns, our Lord Jesus will come "in flaming fire" and in judgment upon his enemies. (2 Thessalonians 1:7-9)

The church shares with Christ in a symbolic three-and-a-half year period of evangelism on the earth. This time is described as *42 months*, and *1,260 days*, and *a time and times and half a time*—each period equaling three-and-a-half years. When severe persecution comes, the church appears to be defeated and dead, but the tribulation will only be for *"a short time."*[105] Just as Christ was raised from the dead, the church will come back to life in a spiritual resurrection. Christians will have another symbolic three-and-a-half year earthly ministry with Christ.

And I saw thrones, and they sat upon them, and judgment was given to them. And I saw the souls of them who were beheaded for the witness of Jesus and for the word of God, and who had not worshiped the beast, neither his image, neither had received his mark upon their foreheads or in their hands. And they lived and reigned with Christ a thousand years. **20:4** Jesus ascended into heaven, after his earthly ministry, his death, and resurrection (Acts 1:1-11). When the two witnesses had finished their testimony, the beast came up out of the bottomless pit and killed them. After being dead, they were resurrected and ascended into heaven just like their Lord (Rev. 11:7-12). Under the fifth seal, John saw "under the altar *the souls* of them who were slain for the word of God." (Rev. 6:9) And now in this vision, John saw *"the souls"* of these slain saints in heaven as they sat on thrones and *"reigned with Christ a thousand years."* (Rev. 20:4) **One thousand is the symbolic number for heaven** (Rev. 7:4). These are symbolic visions of heaven, not heaven itself. They are like the view of heaven in chapters four and five. Just as the twenty-four elders had thrones around the throne of God, the saints having suffered severe persecution are given thrones.

---

[105] Rev. 6:9-11, Rev. 11:7-11, Rev. 12:12, Rev. 20:3-9

Again, we are seeing the long period of evangelism, but this time from heaven's viewpoint. For those who are on the earth, it is a symbolic three-and-a-half year period that corresponds to Christ's earthly ministry. But for the faithful martyrs, the period in which Satan is bound is one thousand years, because it symbolizes the victory they share with Christ when he ascended into heaven. Both the three-and-a-half years and the one thousand years are describing when Satan is bound. These numbers are not to be interpreted literally—they are symbolic!

But the rest of the dead lived not again until the thousand years were finished. This is the first resurrection. 20:5 At the time of the writing of Revelation, the church was figuratively dead due to the severe persecution by Domitian. This persecution ended when Satan was bound and Domitian was assassinated in AD 96. The church was alive again, and the martyrs in heaven had a part in this first symbolic resurrection. The first resurrection is the figurative resurrection of the righteous dead when Satan is bound. When the church is alive and preaching the gospel again on earth, the dead saints are said to be alive and reigning with Christ in heaven. The rest of the dead do not live again until the thousand years are finished. The wicked dead have part in the second resurrection, when persecution against the church is resumed. (Rev. 20:7-9) Ten years later, the Roman Emperor Trajan began persecuting the church again, but for only one year. Satan had been released from the bottomless pit, and wickedness was alive again.

Blessed and holy is he that has part in the first resurrection. On such the second death has no power, but they shall be priests of God and of Christ, and shall reign with him a thousand years. 20:6 He that has part in the first resurrection is alive figuratively and reigning with Christ as the preaching of the gospel is resumed. He is blessed as part of "a royal priesthood" and "holy nation." (1 Peter 2:9)   He that has part in the second resurrection is with Satan in the persecution of God's servants. His ultimate punishment will be "the lake of fire" which is "the second death." (Rev. 20:15) These resurrections are figurative like the one in Ezekiel 37:1-14. In Ezekiel's vision of "The Valley of Dry Bones," God was telling the house of Israel that they would live again as a nation and return to their own land after being dead figuratively in the Babylonian captivity. Ezekiel's vision of a resurrection was not a literal resurrection of dead bodies.

And when the thousand years are expired, Satan shall be loosed out of his prison and shall go out to deceive the nations which are in the four quarters of the earth, Gog and Magog, to gather them together to battle: the number of whom is as the sand of the sea. And they went up on the breadth of the earth and compassed the camp of the saints about, and the beloved city. **20:7-9**   Satan deceives nations throughout the earth to persecute God's servants. These persecutions are not limited to those made by the Roman Empire. Kingdoms and nations, before and after the Romans, have severely mistreated God's people. But God always defeats his enemies!

"Gog and Magog" are symbols for the rulers and nations that persecute God's saints (Rev. 20:8). We read about "Gog of the land of Magog" in Ezekiel 38:2. Magog was a son of Japheth, who was one of the three sons of Noah. (Genesis 10:1-2) The land of Magog is unknown, which lends itself to symbolic use. Gog is described also as "chief prince of Meshech and Tubal." (Ezekiel 38:2-3) KJV, NIV Meshech and Tubal were brothers of Magog. (Gen. 10:2) Meshech's descendants settled in the southeastern part of Asia Minor, which was known as Cilicia in New Testament times. Tubal's descendants

settled in the area of Syria, one of the oldest enemies of Israel.[106]

The Seleucid Dynasty was the last oppressor of God's people before the rise of the Roman Empire. After the death of Alexander the Great, his vast Greek empire was divided among his generals. (Daniel 11:2-4) Seleucus established a kingdom that extended from Persia in the east and to Cilicia in the west. In 301 BC, he founded the city of Antioch in Syria and made it the capital of the Seleucid Dynasty. The eighth king of this dynasty was Antiochus IV, from 175 to 164 BC. He called himself **Epiphanes Theos**, meaning "Illustrious God." He demanded to be worshiped as the incarnation of Jupiter, the chief god of the Romans. He made the temple of God in Jerusalem a shrine to Jupiter and sacrificed "unclean" swine on the temple's altar. The Jewish religion was outlawed, and copies of the Holy Scriptures were destroyed. Over a hundred thousand faithful Jews were killed. Others were sold into slavery. Antiochus IV was the chief prince of Tubal (Syria) and Meshech (Cilicia). He is Gog of the land of Magog in Ezekiel 38:2. He is "the little horn" of the prophecy in Daniel 8:8-25 and the "vile person" predicted in Daniel 11:21. As **Gog**, he serves as a symbol of all persecutors of God's people.

Although greatly outnumbered, Judas Maccabeus and his small group of dedicated Jews fought bravely against the armies of Antiochus IV and defeated them. The temple of God was cleansed three-and-a-half years after its desecration. "I shall not let My holy name be profaned any more. And the nations will know that I am the Lord, the Holy One in Israel." (Ezekiel 39:7) [NASB] In

---

[106] Wright, G. Earnest, *The Westminster Historical Atlas to the Bible*, p. 22, Plate II, The Hebrew Table of Nations and Nelson Beecher Keyes, *Reader's Digest Story of the Bible World*, p. 14

John 10:22, we read of Jesus observing the Feast of Dedication in commemoration of this cleansing of the temple. ***Hanukkah*** is the Hebrew word meaning ***dedication***. Jews throughout the world remember this great victory every December with the celebration of Hanukkah. The first readers of Revelation would have interpreted this reference to "Gog and Magog" in 20:8 as an assurance of victory over Domitian!

And fire came down from God out of heaven and devoured them. **20:9** Christians are given hope in the darkest hour, whenever enemies surround "the camp of the saints and the beloved city." The ***"beloved city"*** is "the New Jerusalem" and is the bride of the Lamb in 21:2-10. The church is the spiritual bride of Christ. (Ephesians 5:25-32) Earthly Jerusalem, a symbol of the old covenant, "is in bondage with her children, but the Jerusalem above is free" and belongs to the new covenant of Christ. (Galatians 4:21-26) The enemies of the church will be destroyed quickly and unexpectedly just as fire destroys. "And I will send fire on Magog ...Then they shall know that I am the Lord." (Ezekiel 39:6) Christ and his church will be victorious over all enemies!

And the devil that deceived them was cast into the lake of fire and brimstone, where the beast and the false prophet are, and shall be tormented day and night for ever and ever. **20:10** The nations that persecuted God's saints were deceived by the devil. These nations are symbolized by the beast, who along with the false prophet, was cast into the lake of fire in Revelation 19:20 at the end of the sixth view. This is proof that the binding of Satan in Revelation 20 does not follow chronologically Revelation 19. The beast would not be around to persecute the saints in Revelation 20:7-9 if he were in the lake of fire. When Satan and the beast are cast into the bottomless pit, they may come out to persecute God's servants. But the lake of fire is a place of eternal torment, and there is no coming out of it.

Christ's return and the final Judgment Day, including the casting of Satan into the lake of fire will not necessarily come during a period of severe persecution against the church. If this were true, Christians would know the Lord would not come during a time of peace. But Jesus said, "Therefore you also be ready, for the Son of Man is coming at an hour you do not expect." (Matt. 24:44) NKJV Christ also may come when things are normal and are going well. "As it was in the days of Noah, so it will be at the coming of the Son of Man. For in the days before the flood, people were eating and drinking, marrying and giving in marriage, up to the day Noah entered the ark; and they knew nothing about what would happen until the flood came and took them all away." (Matt. 24:37-39)NIV Jesus said there would be many signs before the destruction of Jerusalem. (Matthew 24:1-34) But there will be no signs before his Second Coming, when "heaven and earth shall pass away," because "of that day and hour knows no man, no, not the angels of heaven, but the Father only." (Matt. 24:36-37) "But the day of the Lord will come as a thief in the night." (2 Pet. 3:10) A thief gives no signs before he comes; he comes unexpectedly. When you hear people talking about "the signs" of the Lord's coming, you should know that they are misapplying the Scriptures.

Revelation 20:1-10 is the proof text for those who teach that Christ will return to reign on David's throne in Jerusalem for a literal thousand years, **a millennium**. First, notice that this passage says nothing about Christ reigning with living saints on the earth. He is reigning with the souls of dead martyrs in heaven. Second, this theory does not fit the context of the rest of the book. Revelation is full of symbolic language and numbers, not to be taken literally. The numbers in Revelation have symbolic meaning. A thousand is the symbolic number for heaven, not a literal number.

Before the Second Coming of Christ, the cycle of a long period of evangelism and then a short period of persecution will be repeated many times. Satan may be bound in one area of the world and loosed in other places. Jesus promises, "In the world you shall have tribulation; but be of good cheer, I have overcome the world." (John 16:33) When Christ returns, the tribulations will be over, because he will cast Satan and his helpers into the lake of fire, and they will never come out to persecute God's people.

Then John saw *a great white throne and him that sat on it.* **20:11** Jesus Christ is the judge who is seated on the great white throne. Everyone who has ever lived will come before this great throne to be judged. "For we must all appear before the judgment seat of Christ." (2 Cor. 5:10) The throne is white representing the purity and justice of Christ and his judgments. God "has appointed a day in which He will judge the world in righteousness by the Man whom He has ordained. He has given assurance of this to all by raising Him from the dead." (Acts 17:31) NKJV The one who died for us will be our judge.

From whose face, the earth and the heaven fled away, and there was found no place for them. **20:11** When the Lord comes, the earth and the sun, moon, and stars "shall pass away with a great noise" and "be dissolved." (2 Pet. 3:10-12) Our present heaven and earth will disappear and be found no more. Since the earth will vanish at Christ's coming, the doctrine of a thousand-year reign on earth cannot be true.

And I saw the dead, small and great, standing before God. **20:12** The living are not mentioned because this chapter is not about the living, but about the dead.

The faithful *dead* are reigning with Christ for a thousand years in verse 4. "The rest of the *dead* lived not again until the thousand years were finished" in verse 5. Revelation 20 is about the dead. However, 2 Timothy 4:1 teaches that the Lord Jesus Christ "will judge the living and the dead at his appearing."

And the books were opened, and another book was opened, which is the book of life; and the dead were judged out of those things which were written in the books, according to their works. **20:12** Three books will be opened on the Judgment Day. **The Book of Deeds** will be opened because the dead were judged *"according to their works."* Our sinful thoughts and deeds can be removed from this book through the blood of Christ.[107] Do not neglect this great salvation. (Hebrews 2:3) **The Bible** will also be there, because Jesus said that his word "shall judge ... in the last day." (John 12:48) The names of God's faithful children are written in the third book, **the Book of Life.** (Rev. 21:27) The unfaithful will have their names blotted out of the Book of Life. (Rev. 3:4-5)

The sea gave up the dead who were in it; and Death and Hades delivered up the dead who were in them. And they were judged, each one according to his works. **20:13** NKJV When Jesus returns, "all that are in the graves shall hear his voice and shall come forth: those who have done good, unto the resurrection of life and they that have done evil, unto the resurrection of damnation." (John 5:28-29) Jesus said that the believers will be raised "at the last day." (John 6:40) Those who teach the doctrine of the rapture tell us that the righteous dead will be raised over a thousand years before "the last day". Do you believe Jesus or these teachers? Our heaven and earth will pass out of sight when he comes. (2 Peter 3:10-12) Hades, the place of departed spirits, will deliver up the dead to be

---

[107] 1 John 1:7-9, Revelation 1:5, Revelation 7:14

judged along with the living before the great white throne of Christ. According to Jesus, the judgment will be "in the last day." (John 12:48) The resurrection, the destruction of the earth, and the judgment will be in one day—the last day.

***Then Death and Hades were cast into the lake of fire. This is the second death.* 20:14** ^(NKJV) Death and the place of the departed spirits will be no more. "Then comes the end, when he shall have delivered up the kingdom to God, even the Father, when he shall have put down all rule and all authority and power. For he must reign till he has put all enemies under his feet. The last enemy that shall be destroyed is death." (1 Corinthians 15:24-26) When Christ returns, he will destroy death by raising all of the dead on the last day. (John 5:28; John 6:49) He will put down all of his enemies when he judges the living and the dead. (2 Timothy 4:1) When he comes, Christ will **not** begin a millennial reign; instead he will hand over the kingdom to God the Father.

***And whoever was not found written in the book of life was cast into the lake of fire.* 20:15** The second death is the lake of fire, according to verse 14. Those who are not faithful children of God "shall go away into everlasting punishment." (Matthew 25:46) "There shall be wailing and gnashing of teeth." (Matthew 13:42) The lake of fire is the "everlasting fire, prepared for the devil and his angels." (Matthew 25:41) The second death is being separated "from the presence of the Lord, and from the glory of his power." (2 Thessalonians 1:9)

Review Questions on Lesson 12

1. Why is Satan cast into the bottomless pit for a thousand years? 20:1-3 _____

    _____

2. After being bound, Satan will be released for how long?

    _____

3. What will Satan do when he is released? 20:7-8 _____

    _____

4. Whom will the nations surround and seek to destroy? v. 9

    _____

5. In 11:3-7, the _____ was in the bottomless pit when the two witnesses were able to prophesy, but when he came out of the bottomless pit he _____ them.

6. What did the binding of Satan mean to Christians in the first century? _____

7. "A thousand" is the symbolic number for _____.

8. Does Rev. 20 say that Christ will reign on earth? _____

9. Who are said to be alive and reigning with Christ during the thousand years that Satan is bound? v. 4 _____

    _____

10. What is "the first resurrection" in Revelation 20:6?

    _____

11. Why is one "blessed and holy" if he "has part in the first resurrection"? _____

    _____

12. Who would "live again" at the end of the thousand years and have part in the second resurrection? v. 5
    _____

13. What was the resurrection of the dry bones in Ezekiel 37?
    _____

14. What are "Gog and Magog" symbolizing in Rev. 20:8?
    _____

15. What will be the final judgment upon the devil? 20:10
    _____

16. Why are there no signs for Christ's Second Coming?
    _____

17. When John saw the great white throne of the Judgment, what had become of our earth and heaven? v. 11
    _____

18. We shall be judged by the things written in three books; they are The Book of _____, The _____, and The Book of _____.

19. What is the second death? _____

20. Who were cast into the lake of fire? _____
    _____

The Victorious Church
Revelation 21 – 22

And I saw a new heaven and a new earth: for the first heaven and the first earth were passed away. **21:1** John was seeing a symbolic vision of God's dwelling place in heaven.

"God created the heavens and the earth" for man's first home in Genesis 1:1. However, our present earth with its heavens will perish. (Hebrews 1:10-12) "The day of the Lord will come as a thief in the night; in which the heavens shall pass away with a great noise, and the elements shall melt with fervent heat; the earth also and the works that are therein shall be burned up." (2 Peter 3:10) In this seventh view, before the Judgment Day, "the earth and the heaven fled away, and there was found no place for them." (20:11) Our present earth and its heavens are gone when we come to chapter 21; they have disappeared from sight. Time has come to an end. The devil and the wicked have been cast into the lake of fire.

Now John sees a *new* heaven and a *new* earth. The Greek word translated *"new"* means "of a different nature from what is contrasted as old"[108] and as to substance "of a new kind."[109] Thus, John sees a home for man that is totally new.

After informing us that our present universe will be dissolved, Peter adds, "Nevertheless we, according to his promise, look for new heavens and a new earth wherein dwells righteousness." (2 Peter 3:13) The Lord promised in Isaiah 65:17, "For, behold, I create new heavens and a new earth." This promise is completely fulfilled in our

---

[108] W. E. Vine, *Vine's Expository Dictionary of Biblical Words,* p.430
[109] Joseph Henry Thayer, *Thayer's Greek-English Lexicon*, p. 317

eternal home in heaven, after being typically fulfilled in the Jews' return from exile in 536 BC and being spiritually fulfilled now in the church. Peter and his fellow Christians had been "born again" (1 Peter 1:23) and were enjoying "all things that pertain to life and godliness" (2 Peter 1:3), but they still were looking "for new heavens and a new earth." (2 Peter 3:13)

And there was no more sea. 21:1 This statement signifies the removal of all wickedness. The sea is a symbol for the ungodly human masses of the earth that are driven by the tempest of sinful passions and lusts. The beast that persecutes God's servants and supports the harlot Babylon comes up out of the sea. (13:1-8) Babylon "sits on many waters," which "are peoples, multitudes, nations, and tongues." (17:3-15) The wicked will not be found in the new heaven and the new earth. (Rev. 21:8, 21; Rev. 22:14, 15)

And I, John, saw the holy city, New Jerusalem, coming down from God out of heaven, prepared as a bride adorned for her husband. 21:2 The church is the bride of Christ. (Eph. 5:22-32) The New Jerusalem, the holy city, is the Lamb's wife. (21:9, 10) The marriage supper of Christ is being described again, for the bride is coming to the home of her husband, who has prepared a place for her in his Father's house. (19:9; John 14:2-3) The "heaven" through which the holy city is coming down is the new heaven of the new earth. John is seeing the church coming to be with Christ in his heavenly home. The church is "from God" because he is the Creator of the church. God revealed the truth upon which the church is built. (Matthew 16:16-18) God's wisdom is made known by the church, "according to the eternal purpose which he purposed in Christ Jesus our Lord, in whom we have boldness and access with confidence by faith in him." (Ephesians 3:10-12) The saved have been added to the church. (Acts 2:47) Christ "is the mediator of the new testament, that by means of death, for the redemption of the transgressions that were under the first testament, they which are called might receive the promise of eternal inheritance." (Hebrews 9:15) God has prepared a city for Abraham, Isaac, and Jacob because they desired a heavenly country. (Hebrews 11:8-16) The redeemed of all ages will be in the holy city in heaven.

***And I heard a great voice out of heaven saying, "Behold, the tabernacle of God is with men."* 21:3** The Greek word that is translated *tabernacle* may also be translated *home, habitation, or dwelling.* The earthly tabernacle erected by Moses in the wilderness served as a type of the "true tabernacle" in heaven. (Hebrews 8:1-5) Throughout the book of Revelation, symbols from the tabernacle are used to describe heaven.

"And he will dwell with them, and they shall be his people, and God himself shall be with them and be their God."* 21:3** The heavenly community that was in man's original home, the Garden of Eden, will be restored in heaven. Adam and Eve literally walked and talked with God. (Genesis 3:8-13) The promise ***"I will be with you and be your God, and you shall be my people" is made at least fifteen times in the Bible. When God made his covenant with Israel on Mt. Sinai, he said, "If you walk in my statues, and keep my commandments, and do them ... I will set my tabernacle among you ... and I will walk among you, and be your God, and you shall be my people." (Lev. 26:3, 11, 12) When Jeremiah predicted the new covenant, the same promise was made. (Jeremiah 31:31-33; Heb. 8:7-10) God is with his church today in a spiritual way just as he was with Israel under the old covenant, but in heaven God will dwell with his people in person, for "they shall see his face." (Rev. 22:4) Being with God will be the greatest blessing of heaven.

"And God shall wipe away all tears from their eyes; and there shall be no more death, neither sorrow, nor crying, neither shall there be any more pain, for the former things have passed away." 21:4 This is further proof that heaven is being described. Now in the church we are to *"weep with those who weep"* (Romans 12:15), but in heaven there will be no more sorrow and crying. All of the suffering and death of our present earth will be gone.

John had seen the vision of the great multitude in heaven. (7:9-17) The redeemed of all nations were before the throne of God, serving him and praising him for their salvation. And the vision concluded with these words, ***"and God shall wipe away all tears from their eyes."*** Tears will be wiped away in heaven. This again proves that we are seeing parallel views of the victorious church.

Some people think they could not enjoy heaven if a loved one was not there. So, they have concluded that we will not be able to know one another in heaven. During our life on earth, we are able to enjoy the company of family and friends without being sad over the loss of departed loved ones. God may wipe away every tear by keeping us so involved with joyful things there is no place for sadness. We may not recognize each other by the way we will look. Peter, James, and John had never seen Moses and Elijah, but they recognized them on the mount of transfiguration. (Matthew 17:1-4) We will know each other by what we say. Have you not had this experience at homecomings with old friends you had not seen in years? You did not recognize them at first, but you did when they spoke. Our being able to recognize others in heaven will be a great joy. God has the power to blot out all unpleasant things from our memory. If God says he will wipe away all tears, he will do it by whatever means he chooses. Not knowing each other should not be considered as one of the means!

And he that sat upon the throne said, "Behold, I make all things new." And he said to me, "Write, for these words are true and faithful." **21:5** The church now enjoys this blessing in a spiritual sense, but in heaven the blessing will be complete. God is with us spiritually today (Heb. 13:5), but in heaven we shall see him face to face. (22:4) "If anyone is in Christ, he is a new creation; old things have passed away; behold, all things have become new." (2 Cor. 5:17) ᴺᴷᴶⱽ But there are still more new things to come. There will be "a new heaven and a new earth." We still have our old body that is subject to pain and death, but we will receive a new body when Christ comes.[110]

And he said to me, "It is done." **21:6** All of the promises of God have been fulfilled! His eternal purpose has been accomplished. The gathering of his children to his eternal home has been completed. Indeed, all things have been made new.

"I am Alpha and Omega, the beginning and the end. I will give to him who is thirsty of the fountain of the water of life freely." **21:6** God creates and brings to an end. He is the beginning and the end of time. Only God can satisfy the spiritual thirst of man's soul. Jesus taught this important lesson to the Samaritan woman at Jacob's well in John 4:7-14.

"He who overcomes shall inherit all things, and I will be his God and he shall be my son." **21:7** "Every good gift and every perfect is from above and comes down from the Father." (James 1:17) If every good thing you enjoy in this life is from God, just think of your inheritance as his child. He who overcomes the trials and temptations of this world will inherit all things that are good—all the blessings of heaven! There is no other

---

[110] 1 Corinthians 15:50-54, Philippians 3:20-21, 1 John 3:1-2

inheritance so great! In most cases, the earthly father dies before the son receives an inheritance. Your heavenly Father will give you all things in his home for an inheritance, and he will live with you forever—the greatest gift of all! Romans 8:17 promises, "If children, then heirs; heirs of God, and joint heirs with Christ; if so be that we suffer with him, that we may be also glorified together." The heavenly community is being described again with the words, **"I will be his God, and he shall be my son."**

"But the fearful, and unbelieving, and the abominable, and murderers, and whoremongers, and sorcerers, and idolaters, and all liars shall have their part in the lake which burns with fire and brimstone, which is the second death." 21:8 The eternal punishment of the unbeliever is contrasted with the blessings of the faithful. One cannot be *faithful* (full of faith), if he is *fearful* (full of fear). The unfaithful at Pergamos and Thyatira were afraid of the consequences if they refused to engage in the emperor worship and the sinful social activities of their community. (Rev. 2:12-24) All liars will be with Satan, their father. (John 8:44) Those who have loved the falsehoods of the world will have their part in hell along with the wicked, while those who have loved the truth of the Lord will enjoy the glories of heaven with the righteous. This is another proof that Revelation 21 is about the church in heaven.

Then one of the seven angels who had the seven bowls filled with the seven last plagues came to me and talked with me, saying, "Come, I will show you the bride, the Lamb's wife." 21:9 NKJV One of these seven angels had shown John the judgment of the great harlot Babylon in Revelation 17:1. Now in contrast, the Lamb's wife is presented to John in her glory.

And he carried me away in the spirit to a great and high mountain, and showed me that great city, the holy Jerusalem, descending out of heaven from God, having the glory of God. **21:10-11** John was seeing a vision, as indicated by his being "carried away in the spirit." It was a symbolic vision. When the angel showed him the Lamb's wife, John saw the great city, the holy Jerusalem. Since the church is Christ's spiritual wife (Eph. 5:30-32), the church is the New Jerusalem. The holy Jerusalem in heaven is contrasted with the sinful Jerusalem on earth.[111] As the victorious church was descending and approaching God's throne in heaven (verses 2-5), the angel carried John away to a high mountain to get a better view of the glorious city. Christ gave himself for the church, "that He might sanctify and cleanse her with the washing of water by the word, that He might present her to Himself a glorious church." (Ephesians 5:25-27) NKJV

Having the glory of God ... her light was like unto a stone most precious, even like a jasper stone, clear as crystal. **21:11** Since the city has the glory of God, her light is compared to a jasper stone, which also describes God on his throne in Revelation 4:3. The jasper stone is clear as crystal, representing God's purity and holiness.

The holy Jerusalem, the church in heaven, *had a wall great and high, and had twelve gates, and at the gates twelve angels, and names written thereon, which are the names of the twelve tribes of the children of Israel: on the east three gates, on the north three gates, on the south three gates, and on the west three gates. And the wall of the city had twelve foundations, and in them the names of the twelve apostles of the Lamb.* **21:12-14** The number *twelve* is symbolic for God's people. In the Old Testament period, God revealed his covenant on Mount Sinai to the twelve tribes of Israel. On Pentecost, Christ's

---

[111] Revelation 11:8, Galatians 4:24-26, Hebrews 12:22, Philippians 3:20

twelve apostles announced the new covenant. Christians "are fellow citizens with the saints and of the household of God; and are built upon the foundation of the apostles and prophets, Jesus Christ himself being the chief corner stone." (Ephesians 2:19-20) The twenty-four elders around God's throne (4:4) represent the faithful leaders of the twelve tribes of the Old Testament and the twelve apostles of the New Testament. The holy city is composed of God's people, the redeemed of all times.

And he that talked with me had a golden reed to measure the city, the gates thereof, and the wall thereof. 21:15 The angel had a golden reed to measure, which is a symbol of protection. (See comments on Rev. 11:1)

And the city lies foursquare, and the length is as large as the breadth. And he measured the city with the reed, twelve thousand furlongs. The length and the breadth and the height of it are equal. 21:16 The city is a cube in shape, symbolizing the presence of God. In both the tabernacle and the temple, the Most Holy Place had the same length, width, and height and represented God's presence. It also was called "the inner sanctuary." In the temple, it measured twenty cubits long, twenty cubits wide, and twenty cubits high. (1 Kings 6:6-20) In all its dimensions, the sanctuary of the temple was exactly double the size of the tabernacle. The inner sanctuary of the tabernacle was ten cubits, and consequently an exact cube.[112] The Most Holy Place in the tabernacle was 10 cubits long, 10 cubits wide and 10 cubits high. So, **a thousand** is the number that represents **heaven**, God's dwelling place. The number ten is a complete and perfect number. We have ten fingers and ten toes. Ten Commandments were given to Israel. Complete perfection is ten times ten times ten. God's tabernacle (not the temple) in verse three is with men,

---

[112] William Smith, *A Dictionary of the Bible*, p. 664

because the Most Holy Place in the tabernacle measured ten times ten times ten, equaling a thousand, the symbolic number for heaven. The symbolism from the tabernacle can be seen throughout Revelation.

The city measured *"twelve thousand furlongs."* It is a mistake to convert this measurement into miles. Twelve thousand is also a symbolic number. In the Greek, it is "twelve thousand ***stadia***." The length is not important. The number is important! Twelve thousand is symbolic for God's people (12) in heaven (1,000).

And he measured the wall thereof, a hundred and forty and four cubits, according to the measure of a man, that is, of the angel. **21:17** The twelve gates in the wall represent God's people of the Old Testament and the twelve foundations are standing for God's people of the New Testament. (21:12-14) Twelve times twelve is one hundred and forty-four. One hundred and forty-four is a symbolic number for all of God's people. The great high wall and its being measured symbolize protection for God's people.

The construction of its wall was of jasper; and the city was pure gold, like clear glass. **21:18** NKJV The wall of jasper shows the purity and holiness of the church. The city of pure gold describes its beauty and blessings. We have never seen crystal clear jasper (verse 11) and gold that is like clear glass. Heaven is more beautiful than any earthly description.

And the foundations of the wall of the city were garnished with all manner of precious stones. **21:19-20** These precious stones may symbolize the miraculous gifts that were given to the apostles that enabled them to lay the sure foundation of the church. (Ephesians 2:20, 1 Corinthians 3:10-11, Mark 16:20, 1 Thessalonians 1:5, Hebrews 2:3-4)

***The twelve gates were twelve pearls; each individual gate was of one pearl. And the street of the city was pure gold, like transparent glass.* 21:21** ᴺᴷᴶⱽ In New Testament times, pearls were extremely valuable. Jesus compared the blessings of the kingdom of heaven to the worth of one pearl that caused a man to sell everything he had to buy it. (Matthew 13:45-46) No single pearl on earth is large enough to make a city gate. The pearly gates and the street of transparent gold are blessings beyond our human experience.

***And I saw no temple therein: for the Lord God Almighty and the Lamb are the temple of it.* 21:22** The temple represented God's dwelling place. (2 Kings 8:27-30) The holy city does not need a temple to represent God's presence. God is with the New Jerusalem in heaven. Jesus promised in 3:12, "He who overcomes, I will make him a pillar in the temple of My God. ... And I will write on him the name of My God and the name of the city of My God, the New Jerusalem." ᴺᴷᴶⱽ The church is called the temple of God in 1 Corinthians 3:16. God is living with his people in his spiritual temple of heaven.

***And the city had no need of the sun, neither of the moon, to shine in it: for the glory of God did lighten it, and the Lamb is the light thereof.* 21:23** God is the source of light. (Genesis 1:3) Christ, the eternal Word, is "the light of men" and "the true Light, which gives light to every man." (John 1:1-9) God's glory will give light to the city. The sun and the moon belong to the old heaven and the old earth that have passed away.

***And the nations of them which are saved shall walk in the light of it, and the kings of the earth do bring their glory and honor into it.* 21:24** The saved in heaven will come from many nations, not a literal 144,000 from the one nation of physical Israel. (7:3-17) God promised Abraham, "In your seed shall **all the nations** of the earth be blessed." (Gen. 22:18) *"The promise"* is completely fulfilled in heaven. (Galatians 3:7-29) That all nations shall be blessed in Christ is the theme of the Bible. Kings of the earth, such as Melchizedek, David, Hezekiah, and Josiah will be in heaven. One of the blessings of heaven will be the privilege of getting to know great men and women of all times.

And the gates of it shall not be shut at all by day: for there shall be no night there. And they shall bring the glory and the honor of the nations into it. 21:25-26 Ancient cities had gates that were shut whenever enemies came up against them. The gates of this heavenly city do not need to be shut because all enemies have been destroyed, including the devil, who has been cast into the lake of fire. (20:10) The gates also were shut at night due to the dangers of darkness. Darkness is a symbol of sin and evil. (1 John 1:5-7) Night also may stand for death as in John 9:4. The gates will not be shut because there is no sin or death to threaten the city of God. The open gates symbolize the *"access"* to heaven that has been accomplished in Christ Jesus our Lord, *"according to the eternal purpose."* (Eph. 3:11-12) **The glory and honor of the nations** are those who have been redeemed by the blood of Christ and have been servants of righteousness. (Rom. 6:17-23) They have been the salt of the earth and the light of the world. (Matthew 5:13-14) They have glorified God in their minds and bodies. (1 Cor. 6:20) The best of mankind will be in heaven.

And there shall in no wise enter into it anything that defiles, neither whatsoever works abomination or makes a lie, but they which are written in the Lamb's book of life. 21:27 The absence of the wicked will add to the joy of heaven. (Galatians 5:19-21) There will be no fear of thieves or murderers. (Matthew 6:20; Rev. 21:8) There will be no fear of drunkards, drug addicts, or rapists. There will be no exposure to impurity, idolatry or lies. Only the pure in heart shall see God. (Matt. 5:8) Only the true children of God, whose names are written in the Lamb's Book of Life, will be permitted to enter the holy city.

***And he showed me a pure river of water of life, clear as crystal, proceeding out of the throne of God and the Lamb.* 22:1** Man needs water to live, and he needs pure water to be healthy. God is the source of our life and well-being. Christ gives **living water**. (John 4:10; John 7:37-38) There is an abundance of this pure water of life, for it is a river.

***In the midst of the street of it, and on either side of the river, was the tree of life, which bare twelve kinds of fruits, and yielded her fruit every month: and the leaves of the tree were for the healing of the nations.* 22:2** The tree of life is a symbol for eternal life in fellowship with God. When sin entered the world, man lost his right to the tree of life (Gen. 3:22-24), but in heaven that right is restored. (22:14) The trees of the city are of one kind—the tree of life. They line the middle of its street and are on either side of the river of life. This is a most unusual tree; it has "twelve kinds of fruits"—providing complete spiritual nourishment. A comparison may be made to the fruit of the Spirit which is "love, joy, peace, longsuffering, kindness, goodness, faithfulness, gentleness, and self-control." (Gal. 5:22) ^{NKJV} The fruit is always in plentiful supply, since each tree is bearing its fruit every month. The leaves heal all wounds and sufferings that man may have received during his hardships, trials, and persecutions while on earth. In heaven every need will be filled—water, food, and health.

***And there shall be no more curse, but the throne of God and of the Lamb shall be in it, and his servants shall serve him.* 22:3** Man has suffered the curse of being separated from God because of his sins. (Isaiah 59:2;

Genesis 3:22-24) In heaven, the curse will be removed. The redeemed will be in the presence of God, and they will serve him. The fellowship with God that had been in the Garden of Eden will be restored.

And they shall see his face, and his name shall be in their foreheads. **22:4** The privilege of seeing God the Father has been denied us. "No man has seen God at any time; the only begotten Son, who is in the bosom of the Father, he has declared him" (John 1:18); but in heaven we shall see his face. John wrote, "Behold, what manner of love the Father has bestowed upon us, that we should be called the sons of God. Beloved, now we are the sons of God, and it does not yet appear what we shall be: but we know that when he shall appear, **we shall be like him, for we shall see him as he is**." (1 John 3:1, 2) Christ "will transform our lowly body to be like his glorious body." (Philippians 3:21) ᴱˢⱽ God does have a body, for "we shall be like him." We will not have a flesh and blood body, but a heavenly body. (1 Cor. 15:35-53 and 2 Cor. 5:1-8) The greatest blessing of heaven is being with God and seeing his face. *His name shall be in their foreheads.* This is figurative language showing that we belong to him as members of his family. (Rev. 7:2-3; Rev. 14:1) God will be the center of our thoughts. We may conclude that any person who does not want to center his life on God does not want to go to heaven. Anyone who does not enjoy worshiping God would be unhappy and bored in heaven, because heaven is all about praising and serving God.

And there shall be no night there; and they need no candle, neither light of the sun, for the Lord God gives them light. And they shall reign for ever and ever. **22:5** Night, as a symbol of death, is contrasted with the eternal life of God's family. See comments on 21:23 and 21:25 for God's providing the light.

The angel said to me, "These words are trustworthy and true. The Lord, the God of the spirits of the prophets, sent his angel to show his servants the things that must soon take place." 22:6 ^{NIV} The conclusion of the book begins with this verse. The angel who has been showing John the New Jerusalem is still speaking to him. (Rev. 21:9) His words are trustworthy because he received the Revelation from Jesus Christ, who is "the faithful and true witness." (Rev. 3:14) The angel testifies to the truthfulness of the entire book of Revelation, which reveals things that would shortly take place. (Rev. 1:1) Domitian's persecution of Christians would come to an end soon. The prophecies of Revelation are reliable because God, who inspired the holy prophets, made them.

"Behold, I come quickly! Blessed is he that keeps the sayings of the prophecy of this book." 22:7 Next, John hears the voice of Jesus promising to come quickly or suddenly. Figuratively, he comes in natural events and judgments upon persecutors and other sinners from time to time. On the last great day of the Lord, he will come in person as a thief, unexpectedly. The Christian will be blessed if he is prepared for the Lord's coming, whenever he comes.

And I, John, saw these things, and heard them. And when I had heard and seen, I fell down to worship before the feet of the angel who showed me these things. 22:8 John testifies to what he had seen and heard. Being filled with reverential awe at these marvelous things, John fell down to worship before the angel. This seems to be a human reaction when in the presence of one sent by God. He had made this mistake before in 19:10, and so had Cornelius in Acts 10:25-29.

Then he said to me, "See that you do not do that. I am your fellow servant, and of your brethren the prophets, and of those who keep the words of this book.

Worship God." **22:9** ᴺᴷᴶⱽ The angel would not allow John to worship him, because angels are fellow servants of God along with the prophets and other faithful children of God. Just as men are created beings so are the angels. Only God is to be worshiped. This is proof that Jesus Christ is not a created being, but eternal in nature like the Father and the Holy Spirit. The Lamb is to be worshiped.

And he said to me, "Seal not up the sayings of the prophecy of this book; for the time is at hand." **22:10** Daniel was instructed to "seal up" a vision that he had seen, because it concerned the distant future. (Daniel 8:26) The words of Revelation are not to be sealed up because most of its prophecies concerned the period of the Roman Empire. Some of its prophecies were fulfilled within a year, like the death of Domitian. Even the prophecies of heaven would give encouragement to those living in the first century.

"He that is unjust, let him be unjust still; and he which is filthy, let him be filthy still; and he that is righteous, let him be righteous still; and he that is holy, let him be holy still." **22:11** Let a wicked person remain in his wickedness, if the warnings and judgments of this book do not move him to repentance. His hardened heart will condemn him on the Day of Judgment. There will be no additional revelation. Let the righteous remain faithful and be assured by the promises of God.

"And, behold, I come quickly; and my reward is with me, to give to every man according as his work shall be." **22:12** Christ is speaking again. Whenever Jesus comes, it is always quickly or suddenly, whether in temporal judgments or in the final judgment at the end of time. When John was writing Revelation, the future looked hopeless for Christians. They were suffering persecution in various ways. However, things would quickly change when Domitian was killed. Christians

would rejoice in their freedom to preach and worship openly again. Those who had worshiped and followed Domitian would mourn. Jesus said, *"Therefore be ye also ready, for in such an hour as you think not the Son of man comes."* (Matthew 24:44)

"I am Alpha and Omega, the beginning and the end, the first and the last." **22:13** God the Father, who is on the throne, also described himself as "Alpha and Omega" in 21:5-6. Jesus Christ has the same essence, attributes, and eternal divine nature as the Father.

"Blessed are they that do his commandments, that they may have right to the tree of life, and may enter in through the gates into the city." **22:14** The better manuscripts read, *"Blessed are those who wash their robes."* If this is the case, Jesus is still speaking and is pronouncing a blessing on those who have washed their robes in his blood and made them white. (Rev. 7:14) Christ has redeemed them. They have the right to eternal life and the blessings of the heavenly city. John writes, "And this is the record, that God has given to us eternal life, and this life is in his Son. He that has the Son has life; and he that has not the Son of God has not life." (1 John 5:11-12)

"But outside are dogs and sorcerers and sexually immoral and murderers and idolaters, and whoever loves and practices a lie." **22:15** NKJV The greatest curse of hell is being separated from God. They "shall be punished with everlasting destruction from the presence of the Lord and from the glory of his power." (2 Thess. 1:9) A person does not have to be an idolater, sexually immoral, or a criminal to be in this group that is on the outside. He only needs to love and practice a lie. Perhaps the biggest lie people tell themselves is that they do not need God in their lives; they can make it on their own without God telling them what to do. In

2 Thessalonians 2:10-12, we read about those "that perish, because they received not the love of the truth, that they might be saved. And for this cause God shall send them strong delusion, that they should believe a lie: that they all might be damned who believed not the truth, but had pleasure in unrighteousness."

"I, Jesus, have sent my angel to testify to you these things in the churches." **22:16** Jesus testifies to the truthfulness of the angel's words to the churches.

"I am the root and the offspring of David, the bright and morning star." **22:16** In recognition of his royal lineage, Jesus was called "the root of David" when he was the only one who could open the scroll with seven seals. (Rev. 5:5) Christ now reigns as King over his spiritual kingdom, the church, which includes all nations. This is the fulfillment of Isaiah 11. (Romans 15:12; Acts 2:29-36) Jesus is the bright and morning star that brings the hope of the dawning of a new day. (Num. 24:17; 2 Peter 1:19)

And the Spirit and the bride say, "Come." And let him that hears say, "Come." And let him that is athirst come. And whosoever will, let him take the water of life freely. **22:17** Following Jesus' testimony, John begins his closing words with an invitation. The Holy Spirit through Christ's bride, the church, invites everyone to come to Jesus Christ for eternal life. John encourages each individual who hears and obeys the gospel to invite others to come. He who thirsts for righteousness shall be filled. (Matt. 5:6) Isaiah had prophesied, "Everyone who thirsts, come to the waters; and you who have no money, come, buy and eat. Yes, come, buy wine and milk without money and without price." (Isaiah 55:1) [NKJV] Jesus said, "If any man thirsts, let him come unto me and drink." (John 7:37) Only Jesus can satisfy our spiritual thirst. The invitation is freely given to all, but each person who desires the blessing must come to Jesus.

For I testify unto every man that hears the words of the prophecy of this book: If any man shall add to these things, God shall add to him the plagues that are written in this book. And if any man shall take away from the words of the book of this prophecy, God shall take away his part out of the book of life, out of the holy city, and from the things which are written in this book. **22:18-19** Similar warnings are throughout the Bible. "You shall not add to the word which I command you nor take from it, that you may keep the commandments of the Lord your God which I command you." (Deuteronomy 4:2) NKJV Aaron's sons Nadab and Abihu were consumed with fire from the Lord when "they offered **unauthorized** fire before the Lord, contrary to his command." (Leviticus 10:1-2) NIV In Proverbs 30:5-6, we are reminded, "Every word of God is pure; he is a shield to them that put their trust in him. Add you not to his words, lest he reprove you, and you be found a liar." The apostle Paul warned, "But though we, or an angel from heaven, preach any other gospel to you than that which we have preached to you, let him be accursed." (Galatians 1:8)

He who testifies these things says, "Surely I come quickly." Amen. Even so, come, Lord Jesus. **22:20** Jesus is the one who testifies to these things and says that he is coming suddenly. John welcomes the coming of the Lord, whether in a figurative coming that would soon bring deliverance from persecution or in his literal Second Coming at the end of time. Can you say, "Amen"—let it be so? Are you ready for him to come?

The grace of our Lord Jesus Christ be with you all. Amen. **Revelation 22:21**

Review Questions on Lesson 13

1. John saw a _____ heaven and a _____ earth. 21:1

2. What had happened to our present heaven and earth? 21:1 _____ (cf. 20:11)

3. "There was no more sea" in 21:1 signifies the removal of all _____.

4. The _____ _____ was "prepared as a bride adorned for her husband." 21:2

5. Who is the bride of Christ? _____

6. "And they shall be his _____, and God himself shall be _____ them and be their _____." 21:3

7. "And God shall wipe away all _____." 21:4

8. What four things will be "no more" in Revelation 21:4?
   _____

9. He who overcomes "shall inherit _____ _____."

10. While God's people are enjoying heaven, where will the "fearful, unbelieving, abominable ... and all liars" be?
    _____

11. The Lamb's wife is described as "the great city, the holy _____" 21:9-10

12. The holy city had how many gates? _____

13. The wall of the city had _____ foundations.

14. What is the symbolic number for God's people? _____

15. The holy city is a _____ in shape, symbolizing the _____ of God.

16. The symbolic number for heaven is _____.
    Why? _____

17. The city measured _____ stadia (furlongs).
    What does this measurement symbolize?
    _____

18. "The city was pure _____, like unto clear _____."

19. The temple and light of the city are _____
    and the _____.

20. "And the nations of them which are _____ shall walk
    in the light" of the holy city. 21:24

21. What was proceeding out of the throne of God? 22:1
    _____

22. What does the tree of life symbolize? 22:2
    _____

23. "And there shall be no more _____." 22:3

24. God's servants shall see God's _____. 22:4

25. The angel who had revealed this vision of heaven said,
    "These words are _____ and _____."

26. John was told to worship only _____ when he fell down
    to worship before the feet of an angel.

27. Who is speaking in Revelation 22:12-16? _____

28. The _____ and the _____ say, "Come!" and
    take the water of life freely.

29. We are not to _____ or _____ the things
    written in this book.

30. When Jesus said, "Surely I come quickly," what was John's
    response? _____

The Unity of Revelation | 211
The Key is Revelation 1:18

"I am He who lives"	"and was dead"	"behold, I am alive"
Long Period of Evangelism	**Short Period of Tribulation**	**Judgment and Victory**
For 3 ½ years Jesus preached with opposition.	For 3 days Jesus was in the tomb, future appeared hopeless.	After 3 days Jesus resurrected and victorious!

Revelation 1:9
The church was "in the tribulation."

Revelation 6:1-8 White Horse of Evangelism	Revelation 6:9-11 Slain Saints a little time	Revelation 6:12-17 Judgment upon the enemies of God
Revelation 11:3-6 The two witnesses were **alive** for 3 ½ years.	Revelation 11:7-10 The two witnesses were **dead** for 3 ½ days.	Revelation 11:11-13 The two witnesses **alive again** and victorious!
Revelation 12:6 Church is fed 1,260 days or **3 ½ years.**	Revelation 12:12 Devil has great wrath. **Nero's persecution** "a short time"	Revelation 12:13-14 Church is given wings of eagle to **victory!**
Revelation 12:14-16 Church is fed **3 ½ years** with opposition.	Revelation 12:17 Satan makes war. **Domitian's persecution** Revelation being written	
Revelation 13:5 Church is blasphemed. 42 months or **3 ½ years.**	Revelation 13:7 The beast, Domitian, makes war against the saints for **one literal year.**	Revelation 14:1 Christ & Church are victorious! Their enemies are **judged**.
Revelation 20:1-6 **Satan is bound for 1,000 years** and cast into the bottomless pit to keep him from persecuting saints.	Revelation 20:7-9 **Satan is released** "for a little while," and he deceives the nations to persecute the saints.	Rev. 20:9 – 22:15 **Satan is judged.** He & his followers are cast into the lake of fire. **The church is victorious.**

NOTES

Bibliography

Addison-Wesley. ***World History Traditions and New Directions.*** Addison-Wesley Publishing Company, 1991.

Barnes, Albert. ***Barnes Notes***. Biblesoft

Bruce, F. F. ***The Spreading Flame***. Grand Rapids, Michigan: Wm. E. Erdmans Publishing Co., 1961.

Butler, Paul T., ***Daniel,*** Joplin: Missouri, College Press, 1982

Cox, Frank L. ***Revelation in 26 Lessons***. Nashville, TN: Gospel Advocate Company, 1967.

Farrar, Lucian, Jr. ***The Book of Daniel, "The Most High Rules".*** Tulsa, OK: James Kay Publishing, 2014.

Halley, Homer. ***Revelation: An Introduction and Commentary.*** Grand Rapids: Baker Book House, 1979.

Hendriksen, William. ***More Than Conquerors***. Grand Rapids, MI: Baker Book House, 1952.

Hull, Edward, ***The Wall Chart of World History***. Dorset Press, 1988.

Jones, Joe D. ***Victory in Jesus***. Searcy, AR: 1990.

Keil & Delitzsch. ***Commentary of the Old Testament.*** Biblesoft

Keyes, Nelson Beecher. ***Story of the Bible World***. Pleasantville, NY: The Reader's Digest Association, Inc., 1962.

Latourette, Kenneth Scott. ***A History of Christianity.*** New York: Harper & Brothers, 1953.

Maier, Paul L. ***Eusebius—The Church History.*** Grand Rapids, MI: Kregel Publications, 1999.

Marlin, J. T. ***The Seven Churches of Asia***. Nashville, TN: Williams Printing Company, 1980.

Mattox, F. W. ***The Eternal Kingdom***. Delight, AR: Gospel Light Publishing Company, 1961.

McCord, Hugo. *McCord's New Testament Translation.* Sweet Home, TX: World English School, Inc., 1989.

McGarvey, J. W. *The Fourfold Gospel.* Cincinnati: The Standard Publishing Foundation.

North, Stafford. *Unlocking Revelation.* Nashville, TN: 21st Century Christian, 2003.

Pack, Frank. *Revelation.* Austin, TX: Sweet Publishing Company, 1965.

Price, Ross. *The Wycliffe Bible Commentary.* Nashville, TN: The Southwestern Company, 1968.

Roberts, J. W. *The Revelation to John (The Apocalypse).* Austin, TX: Sweet Publishing Company, 1974.

Roper, David. *Truth for Today Commentary, Revelation.* Searcy. AR: Resource Publications, 2002.

Shelly, Rubel. *The Lamb and His Enemies.* Nashville, TN: 21st Century Christian Foundation, 1983.

Suetonius. *Lives of the Twelve Caesars.* http://penelope.uchicago.edu/Thayer/E/Roman/Texts/Suetonius/12Caesars/home.html

Summers, Ray. *Worthy is the Lamb.* Nashville, TN: Broadman Press, 1951.

Wallace, Foy E., Jr. *The Book of Revelation.* Nashville, TN: The Foy E. Wallace Jr. Publications, 1966.

Wright, G. Ernest. *The Westminster Historical Atlas to the Bible.* Philadelphia: The Westminster Press, 1956

www.ingramcontent.com/pod-product-compliance
Lightning Source LLC
Chambersburg PA
CBHW060823050426
42453CB00008B/555